All You Can Pay

Also by Anna Bernasek

The Economics of Integrity: From Dairy Farmers to Toyota, How Wealth Is Built on Trust and What that Means for Our Future (2010)

All You Can Pay

*How Companies Use Our Data
to Empty Our Wallets*

ANNA BERNASEK
and
D. T. MONGAN

NATION
BOOKS
New York

Copyright © 2015 by Anna Bernasek and D. T. Mongan.

Published by
Nation Books, A Member of the Perseus Books Group
116 East 16th Street, 8th Floor
New York, NY 10003

Nation Books is a co-publishing venture of the Nation Institute and the
Perseus Books Group.

Books published by Nation Books are available at special discounts for bulk purchases
in the United States by corporations, institutions, and other organizations. For more
information, please contact the Special Markets Department at the Perseus Books Group,
2300 Chestnut Street, Suite 200, Philadelphia, PA 19103, or call (800) 810-4145,
ext. 5000, or e-mail special.markets@perseusbooks.com.

Designed by Milenda Lee

A CIP catalog record for this book is available from the Library of Congress.

ISBN: 978-1-56858-474-4 (HC)
ISBN: 978-1-56858-475-1 (EB)
Library of Congress Control Number: 2015934539

10 9 8 7 6 5 4 3 2 1

To Lily and Natalie

Contents

Introduction

A *Fable for Today*

There was once a town in the heart of America where citizens lived in prosperity and harmony. In that town lived a young family, full of hope and promise, in a small but neatly kept home. In the mornings the children walked to the local elementary school, and the parents headed to work. They spent evenings together after doing homework and sharing a family meal.

The family wasn't rich, but it was prosperous. Work was secure, and together the parents made more than enough money to cover expenses and steadily add a bit to savings. As season followed season, the children blossomed, and the parents glowed with pride.

Material abundance surrounded them. Nearby shops stocked more than anyone could ask for, attractively displayed and carefully labeled at reasonable fixed prices. The supermarket alone stocked thirty thousand items for the household. Whatever wasn't available locally could conveniently be ordered from locations far and wide. Choices had to be made, of course, but a decent income and responsible spending habits covered the necessities, as well as treats like vacations and a few indulgences.

Year followed blissful year, until one day the parents noticed things had changed. Work became a little less secure, and expenses seemed harder to meet. The first shock came in the form of a surprise medical bill that insurance did not cover, followed by a very expensive car repair during an inopportune time when the family was hundreds of miles from home. Next, the mortgage payment rose sharply. At the supermarket, despite incessant promotions and discounts, the final bill always seemed to be higher than expected. Cellular phone and Internet bills occasionally jumped by hundreds of dollars. The price of energy—electricity and heating oil—began to spike inexplicably. Banking and credit-card fees popped up where none had been before. The investment fund holding the family's savings suffered a loss. Worst of all, a drop in their home's value made it worth less than the amount due on the mortgage.

The formerly happy family felt a kind of blight creep into their lives. Where once they had felt security, they now felt festering anxiety. Vague financial concerns coalesced into a gnawing dread of impending need. Rather than saving and getting ahead, the family began to fall behind.

Soon the family couldn't keep within a budget anymore. The price of everything, from milk to mortgages, seemed to shift according to mysterious market forces. A decent portion of the family budget just couldn't be predicted at all. And there arose more and more nasty surprises, such as an item or service costing many times what, in the past, had been considered fair. Every time the parents found a new solution or managed to save a little money, things would change. Once an introductory period for a new product or contract passed, the price would jump before the family even got used to the new arrangement. It seemed nothing was offered on simple fixed terms anymore. There were complicated deals for just about anything. Some businesses charged a definite price but left uncertain what goods or services would actually be delivered. Other products required contracts with penalties and fees that kicked in all the time.

The parents began to have slightly paranoid concerns. They wondered if their smartphones, tablets, and computers were watching them. Aggressive online offers appeared to correspond to private e-mail messages. Search results took into account not just location but other preferences that could only come from intimate knowledge. The price of eggs spiked just before a Sunday brunch party, which seemed odd. And even gasoline seemed to cost more when the family was running late.

The worst of it was, the family felt as if it were on its own. There was no recourse when they made a bad bargain; the terms worked against them in whichever one of the hundreds of service contracts and user agreements the parents had apparently agreed to. They couldn't appeal to the unfairness of it all because they could no longer tell what was fair and didn't even fully understand the terms of what they were buying. It would have been absurd to even think of trying to figure out whether others were receiving similar deals or something different. The only thing they knew for sure was that their friends and neighbors felt anxious too. Meanwhile, a few well-positioned companies seemed to be doing very well indeed.

Our little fable is just that: a fable. But every part of it is, in a sense, true. Millions of consumers have experienced some of the effects described, and more than a few have experienced the majority of them. Businesses throughout the world are learning more and more about how to charge the highest price for their wares and services and how to shift risk off of their own books and onto the backs of customers.

We are not, at least not entirely, the passive victims of a sinister plot. In large part we have done this to ourselves. Like the Algonquins selling all of Manhattan for a few ax-heads and blankets, consumers seem eager to compromise their future in exchange for pennies' worth of service or convenience.

Today we gaze upon the waning days of a great consumer age, standing at the threshold of a new era. Mass markets with low-cost commodity products are quickly disappearing. Huge, well-capitalized firms are amassing more information than ever before conceived. All of the individual building blocks to completely reshape the global consumer economy exist. The techniques are not yet perfected, but change is arriving at the speed of data.

The question for consumers around the world is what will prevail in the market. Will society passively accept the results of a massive data-driven gold rush, in which consumers pay *All You Can Pay*, or will consumers demand a better bargain?

A lot is at stake—not just our personal wealth but something even more important: the continued existence of the free markets we have long enjoyed—perhaps even our ways of life. Fortunately, the result depends on us.

PART I

The Evolution of Markets

1

The Prize

How much would you pay for air? It's an absurd question. After all, air is free. There's no reason to pay for it. Air seems a poor choice for a commercial product. But what if you were in a place with limited air—the top of a mountain, underwater, or in a sealed room? In those places, you'd pay a lot for air, maybe even everything you have.

If not air, then how about water? For a moment water seems absurd too. It's available nearly everywhere, and it's so cheap it's often given away for free. But if you're thirsty and you're out of options, you'll pay plenty for water. Both air and water are so important that after a short time—minutes in the case of air, a few days in the case of water—humans can't live without them. We derive an immense benefit from those plentiful commodities and yet we generally pay very little for them.

The difference between how much you would pay for something if you had to and how much you actually pay in the current market is called *economic surplus*. The story of business, from the very first barter trade right through to the latest financial transaction a millisecond ago, is a story of economic surplus. People and businesses buy or sell goods and services because what they get—whether it's air or a car or a dollar—is worth more to them than what they give in exchange. The difference between what something is worth to you and what you actually give in exchange for it can be very personal. Surplus varies from person to person, from time to time, and from situation to situation.

The surplus captured by consumers is known as the *consumer surplus*, and the profits from businesses are known as the *producer surplus*. The *total economic surplus* is the sum of both the consumer surplus and the producer surplus. The surplus is always up for grabs as consumers try to pay less, get more, and maximize enjoyment while businesses try to charge more, deliver less, and minimize cost.

Take water, for example. In most parts of the world, clean water occurs naturally. Sometimes minor filtration or chemical adjustment is necessary, but unless you're in a spaceship, nobody makes water. Yet despite the fact that water is available from taps throughout the United States for next to nothing, today there exists a $13 billion bottled-water industry that sells water to consumers. Bottled-water companies don't create water; it comes from nature. At the source it could contain a few minerals, maybe even some fizz. Sometimes it's just the same as regular tap water but in a bottle. What the companies have figured out, though, is that people drink water all the time, and it's very important to them. So the bottled-water industry actually sells packaging. Thirsty Americans could easily find a tap nearby if they went to a little trouble, but they'll pay for a bottle from the newsstand at the corner if it's just a bit easier to get. So nearly everywhere, water is sold in convenient resealable bottles. When you think about it, that's all there is to bottled water: a little bit of convenience. And throughout the global beverage market, bottled water is by far the fastest-growing product. Some people—typically those with fewer means or more time—will still seek out taps and drinking fountains, but many others will willingly pay a few dollars for a cup or two of water in a bottle.

The total surplus that could be captured from selling water is probably infinite because nobody can survive for long without it. However, so far nobody has monopolized the product. It's a commodity and it sells into a mass market. Today there are many different brands of bottled water. The creation of the bottled-water industry shows how businesses have figured out ways to charge for something that previously was considered a public good and provided to all at no cost. In effect, bottled-water companies have nibbled away at the consumer surplus by enticing consumers to pay for what they once got for free.

Bringing Water to the Mississippi

The large bottled-water market didn't happen overnight. It began almost half a century ago in New York City when an American marketing genius and a savvy French businessman teamed up to launch America's first successful bottled water. A forty-year-old ambitious marketing executive, Bruce Nevins was on the lookout for the next big thing when he met Gustave Leven. At the outset Nevins was skeptical. Bottled water? From France? It seemed fanciful to get Americans to pay for something that was already piped into their homes.

Deep down, however, Nevins sensed an opportunity. Next to air, water represented the ultimate commodity: cheap, universal, and essential for life. It had inherent value, value without limit. At certain times people would be willing to pay almost anything for it. The trick was how to capture even just a little bit of that value. A small fraction of the value consumers derived from water would add up to a fortune.

It was the mid-1970s, and Nevins had just left Levi Strauss at the top of its game. Every young person around the world, from Moscow to Manila, wanted a pair of Levi's, in part due to Nevins's international marketing efforts. But Nevins possessed an entrepreneurial streak and left it all behind to strike out anew, founding Pony Sporting Goods with a former colleague from Levi Strauss. Through friends, acquaintances, and friends of friends, the pair scrambled to find a group of investors to back the company. One investor, Gustave Leven, was chairman of the board of the French water company Perrier and the man who single-handedly turned a long-forgotten mineral water into one of France's premier brands.

Leven warmed to Nevins immediately. It was Nevins's sense of openness to ideas that initially attracted Leven. The Frenchman was looking for an ally, someone who believed in Perrier as much as he did, and he thought he could convince Nevins to do what many considered impossible at the time: change American habits. Leven believed he could sell bottled water that was distinctly French and foreign to a population accustomed to drinking good old American-made soft drinks like Coke and 7UP.

Leven was as passionate as ever about sparkling water. He had come across Perrier as a young stockbroker right after World War II. After visiting the natural springs where Perrier is sourced in Vergéze in Southern France for a client, he decided to buy the company himself. Perrier boasted a decorated history. A local doctor named Louis Perrier bought the springs in 1898 and operated a spa, offering bottled water for sale. A few years later St. John Harmsworth, a wealthy Englishman, bought the springs and sold Perrier thoughout the British Empire. It was served at Buckingham Palace and became popular with the royal family, making it an instant hit in Britain and earning Perrier a reputation as the "champagne" of waters. But once Harmsworth died and the war started, Perrier languished. Losing its main market and without capital investments, Perrier struggled to produce and sell bottled water. For fourteen years Perrier remained largely abandoned until Leven first visited its springs in the late 1940s. Leven saw an opportunity to resurrect Perrier and seized it. Perrier had been better known in Britain and the colonies than in France, but under Leven, Perrier became France's leading sparkling water. After three decades of growth, Leven believed Perrier was ready for something bigger and bolder, and he turned his sights on launching the bottled water in the huge U.S. market. But first, he needed someone who really knew the ropes.

Leven had been after Nevins for months to take a look at his proposal. But Nevins dragged his feet. McKinsey, the world's leading management consultant, had just done a detailed study about Perrier's prospects in the United States and concluded it wasn't a viable proposition. That seemed to make Leven even more determined, but it only discouraged Nevins. What could Nevins possibly find that McKinsey hadn't?

Nevins finally agreed to do some research. Perrier was already sold in high-end restaurants in Manhattan and Los Angeles but otherwise, at that point, the pear-shaped green bottles were largely ignored, collecting dust on American shelves. Nevins began by conducting focus groups, searching for insights into how to get consumers to buy water. After the first one or two, he became intrigued. There was something there after all, and he could sense a purpose for the product.

In the 1970s a growing health awareness among Americans increasingly drew many to diet drinks. But diet drinks used saccharine, which was believed to be carcinogenic, and that scared a lot of people off. That's when Nevins realized Perrier wasn't in the bottled-water business after all—it was a mistake to think about Perrier in that way. Perrier was actually in the alternative-beverage business, a healthy alternative to everything else out there: soft drinks, diet drinks, and alcohol. What could be not only as healthy to drink as water but also a real pleasure to drink? The bubbles made Perrier seem luxurious without any guilt. Distinctive packaging made it both convenient and unique.

Leven, thrilled that Nevins had become excited about Perrier's American prospects, made Nevins the head of Perrier in the United States. Perrier was officially launched in 1977, first in New York City and then in Los Angeles, San Francisco, Florida, Chicago, and eventually the rest of the country. Nevins coordinated the launch with a splashy ad campaign featuring one of the nation's best-known and most-celebrated stars of the day, Orson Welles. Welles became the face, or rather the voice, of Perrier. At around 350 pounds, Welles remained off camera, narrating the commercial. "Pure Perrier," Welles said in his distinctive voice, "enjoy it in good health. Naturally sparkling water from the center of the earth."

Marathon sponsorships accompanied Perrier's ad campaign. By the late 1970s, thousands of people ran the New York City marathon wearing Perrier T-shirts. At the same time, Nevins worked on the press. He flew a group of American journalists to France to see Perrier for themselves. First in Paris, then at the natural springs where Perrier is sourced, the journalists were treated to the best of everything. But Nevins also worked on making the bottled water affordable. His vision of Perrier did not include champagne prices. He wanted to make Perrier an approachable product for most Americans, so he negotiated shipping prices down, to offer a lower retail price, and sold Perrier in supermarkets around the country.

Perrier became a huge success and has been hailed as one of the great marketing triumphs of the twentieth century. In the first three years, sales of Perrier increased more than 3,000 percent and kept on climbing. By 1988 Americans were buying 300 million bottles of Perrier a year and the company had captured 80 percent of the market. Looking back on it now, Nevins, in his eighties, admits Perrier represented the pinnacle of his career.

So what had Nevins really done? He took springwater, packaged it, shipped it halfway around the world, and convinced many American consumers that water is worth paying for. Imagine selling water to people living on the banks of the Mississippi or the shores of the Great Lakes. Nevins was selling French water very profitably in a country blessed with plentiful water resources of its own. What's more, selling water flew in the face of a long-standing American civic tradition of providing water to everyone for free, or nearly free.

In the process, Nevins captured a piece of the surplus formerly owned by consumers. With his marketing genius, Nevins took over the high end of the market for water: consumers who were willing to pay to get something more than they got from tap water. Formerly, all those Perrier customers drank ordinary water, and the cost of Perrier stayed in their wallets. By communicating his vision of Perrier as an affordable luxury, Nevins captured a part of the greatest prize in business: a portion of the consumer surplus, a sliver of the value consumers derive from water.

A Bottled-Water Industry

With the success of a single product, Nevins touched off an explosion in the beverage industry, paving the way for others to follow. And many brands have followed with great success. Since Perrier first launched, the bottled-water industry has never looked back. After soft drinks and alcohol, bottled water now comprises the third-biggest category of beverages consumed in the United States by number of gallons. It accounted for 17 percent of all beverages consumed in the United States in 2012, ahead of coffee at 15 percent and just behind alcoholic drinks, which had 19 percent of the market.

It's amazing how fast the bottled-water industry has grown. Although soft drinks still make up 27 percent of the entire beverage market, bottled water is catching up. In the past decade, the consumption of bottled water in the United States grew steadily while the consumption of soda fell. Per capita consumption of bottled water increased 50 percent from 2002 to 2012, according to the Beverage Marketing Corporation, while the consumption of soda has declined slightly. Still, Americans overall consume more soda than bottled water: about 30.8 gallons of water versus 47 gallons of soda in a year. But if the trend of increasing bottled-water consumption continues, it won't be long before bottled water outsells soda nationwide. Those in the bottled-water business predict that day may come sooner rather than later. Tim Brown, president and CEO of Nestlé Waters North America, contends that by 2017 Americans will be drinking more bottled water than soft drinks. And he expects that trend to follow all around the world.

It's already happening in the biggest regional market in the United States: the New York metro area, a region of more than 20 million people spanning New York state, Connecticut, and New Jersey. Without a secret formula or a glitzy ad campaign, a single brand of water, Poland Spring, outsells Coke and Pepsi by a huge margin. In 2013, in the New York metro area, sales of all varieties of Coca-Cola added up to $374 million. In comparison, sales of Poland Spring in the same area totaled $507 million. Poland Spring is the only major beverage brand that increased its 2013 sales in the New York metro area. Sales of both Coke and Pepsi declined. Other markets around the country show signs of following. Bottled water outsells soda in supermarkets in fifteen other major U.S. cities, according to the Nielsen Company. That includes Las Vegas, Boston, Dallas, Phoenix, and Houston.

Nevins could never have guessed how big the bottled-water market would eventually become. In fact, it was Nevins who bought Poland Spring for Perrier in the late 1980s. And he admits today that he is as surprised as anyone by America's thirst for bottled water. "We had hoped the US market would catch up to Europe but we never expected it to be a $13 billion business," he says.

So why do Americans buy bottled water when they can drink water virtually for free from the tap? In Perrier's case, the bubbles and the story of its source in France made it unique and enticing. But Perrier itself isn't a premium product—it comes out of the ground for next to nothing. Rainwater and carbon dioxide are naturally forced up through limestone, creating bubbling water, an effect that gave Perrier's source the name *les bouillens*, "boiling waters" in French. In an unadvertised twist, the water and the gas are actually collected separately and then combined back at a bottling plant to provide consistent carbonation. Perrier contains a few naturally occuring minerals: a bit of calcium, potassium, and magnesium as well as about half a dozen or more other minerals in trace amounts. But in essence it's a very simple product. Leven, the French founder of modern-day Perrier, took a low-cost product and marketed it as a luxury. Then Nevins sold that image to Americans. In effect, Leven and Nevins gave consumers who would willingly pay more for water a reason to do so.

Still, or "flat" water as it is also called, is somewhat different, with no bubbles or frills to separate it from what comes out of the tap. Yet today, still water outsells sparkling water around the country. Two of the leading still-water brands in the United States, Dasani and Aquafina, are essentially sourced from the public system. There's virtually nothing unique about the waters themselves.

Pepsi first launched Aquafina back in 1994, and it was so successful that Coca-Cola followed with Dasani just five years later. Both products are sold as purified water. In Dasani's case, Coca-Cola bottling plants around the country collect the water from the most convenient local water source near each plant. Usually, that means connecting to the nearest town's water or, if there isn't running water, using well water. Coca-Cola then filters the water and adds in small quantities of mineral salts for uniform taste. Coca-Cola essentially buys Dasani water from the local source at a very low price, bottles it, and then sells it for a substantial profit.

It's interesting to note that although Americans have no problem buying tap water from Coca-Cola, the same can't be said for Europeans, at least not so far. Dasani's launch in the United Kingdom in 2004 was a disaster. Simply put, the British wouldn't buy Coca-Cola's water. Dasani torpedoed the launch when Fleet Street tabloids ran headlines like "The Real Sting" and "Coke sells tap water for 95p." But mineral contamination that ended up in some of the bottled water is what sealed Dasani's fate in the United Kingdom. Coca-Cola pulled Dasani in the United Kingdom and shelved plans to expand into Europe.

In the United States, some consumers buy Dasani and Aquafina in part due to inchoate fears that tap water and communal taps or fountains are unsafe. Overwhelming evidence points to the contrary, but local water departments don't spend big money marketing their product. Convenience is perhaps an even more important feature of bottled water, though. Coca-Cola isn't selling Americans water; it's really selling Americans a little bit of packaging and ease. In essence, Coca-Cola sells the value of your time—the time it would take to get a bottle, find a tap, and fill it yourself.

The Value of Water

There's nothing wrong with what Coca-Cola does, of course, so long as it misleads no one. Time, as the saying goes, is money. But depending on the situation—whether or not you are in a hurry, how thirsty you are, how many alternatives are for sale, and how near you are to the closest public drinking fountain—you might be willing to pay a lot for water, far more than just a dollar or two. If the price of bottled water went up, you might just pay it. For many Americans, the price of bottled water going up by fifty cents won't affect their consumption much at all. That's not true for everyone, though. For some it would be the straw that breaks the camel's back. The extra cost would push them over a tipping point, and they might switch to a generic brand or give up bottled water entirely in favor of tap. If the price doesn't go up, everyone who could pay more but doesn't have to benefits. The extra money they would be willing to pay stays in their pockets rather than being spent on bottled water. That money is consumer surplus. With annual purchases of bottled water in U.S. supermarkets running in the $13 billion range, the consumer surplus in bottled water alone easily runs into several billion dollars, the amount sellers could get if they could selectively charge higher prices to consumers who would pay more for it.

Another way to think about the consumer surplus is the implied savings a consumer earns when he or she pays less than the maximum price the seller can charge for the product. For a consumer to buy a product, the price must be acceptable: less than the most he or she is willing to pay. As the price increases, at a certain point the consumer becomes indifferent. And beyond that point, he or she doesn't buy. That point of indifference, where a consumer could "take it or leave it," is the maximum price he or she is willing to pay at a given point in time. Anything below that maximum benefits the consumer. And that's the important point about the consumer surplus: It represents money that stays in the consumers' pockets instead of going to the sellers. And that surplus is vast. Someone accustomed to paying $1 for water could pay $200 in the right circumstances. Think of any high-pressure situation—for example, a few minutes before a job interview or an important public speech. There's no time to bargain, and going thirsty is a poor choice. And think of wine. Someone who typically spends ten dollars on a bottle of everyday wine might spend ten times that much to impress a colleague or to celebrate a special occasion with loved ones. The same principle applies, albeit at lower prices, to bottled water.

Since it's essential for life, water of any kind typically has a very large consumer surplus. If we were forced to, we would pay almost anything to survive. Yet typically we pay very little for water. The average American household pays around $335 a year for water. The difference between what we would be willing to pay and what we actually do pay stays in our pockets.

Today Americans will typically part with a dollar or more for a small bottle of water in return for a small amount of convenience. And this trend is growing, particularly as public water fountains become harder to find, failing to keep up with demand. Visitors to Rome can still find street fountains, open taps that serve as reminders of the imperial practice of providing free water to all. New York still has water fountains if you know where to look, but Poland Spring is available on every corner. Before Perrier paved the way, consumers seldom paid for water. Practically the entire value of water remained with consumers rather than businesses. Then Nevins, driven by Leven's vision, used a little marketing magic to create demand for a previously unknown product. Nobody needed Perrier specifically, but the public was taught to appreciate it through a mass-market ad campaign and convenient distribution. Now consumers are accustomed to buying water when and where they want it, and producers make a profit.

The Prize: The Entire Consumer Surplus

A typical grocery store contains 38,000 products, and there's profit and consumer surplus for each one. In fact, consumer surplus is attached to every single product and service in the entire economy, even or perhaps, especially, in things like air that we consume for free. Consume anything and there's a piece of the total surplus up for grabs. Hal Varian, an economist at the University of California, Berkeley, and chief economist at Google, whose microeconomics textbook has been studied by legions of undergraduate economics students over the years, explains the size of the consumer surplus for air. "If you think of the consumer surplus for oxygen, the question to ask is 'how much would you pay for the oxygen you breathe compared to doing without it altogether?' Here the answer is essentially everything you have." When you think about the consumer surplus in those terms, it is profoundly big. The entire consumer surplus is essentially the price of your life.

Yet at any given point in time, the size of the consumer surplus for a specific product can vary. The consumer surplus depends on each person's desires and on their alternatives. At one moment, we might be willing to spend everything we have for a bottle of water—if we were dying of thirst. A moment later, our thirst quenched, we might not want to spend much at all. Stores that sell bottled water know that our circumstances might make us willing to pay considerably more than normal, and they try to set prices accordingly. Think about the cheapest outlets from which to buy bottled water (usually club stores like Sam's Club or discounters like Walmart, or even online bulk sellers). They know customers are not desperate for a drink of water right then and there, and most importantly, they know their customers can shop around and find alternatives if they don't like the price. That's why they tend to offer the best prices around the country for bottled water.

So what's the most expensive place, in general, to buy bottled water? Probably a restaurant. It's impolite to bring your own bottle of water, and it's hard to imagine getting up from the table and running out for Perrier. The airport is probably the second most expensive place to buy water. Once they're past security, where one *can't* take water through, passengers are ripe for the picking. Airport stores know you can't shop around, and they charge accordingly. Water sold at John F. Kennedy International Airport for $3.99 costs $2.00 or less at supermarkets. Convenience stores come next—nobody buys water there unless they want to drink it right away. And few good alternatives to convenience stores exist. Think of freeway stops or amusement parks.

So the price of a bottle of water varies considerably throughout our economy according to the circumstances. The more sellers can charge, the greater surplus they receive. Therefore the consumer surplus, an almost limitless quantity, is the ultimate prize for firms.

The tussle over the consumer surplus and the producer surplus has been a reality of the commercial world for as long as markets have been around. But Alfred Marshall, a British economist, first articulated and formalized the concept. Marshall explained the idea of the producer surplus and consumer surplus as part of his major work *Principles of Economics*, published in 1890. In that groundbreaking book, Marshall developed the basic supply-and-demand diagrams that both economics students and professionals still use today to understand particular firms or industries. His now instantly recognizable scissor-like diagrams of a downward-sloping demand curve and an upward-sloping supply curve form the basic understanding of microeconomics and incorporate ideas often taken for granted today, such as the equilibrium price, the demand elasticity, the law of diminishing utility, and the marginal utility. "Marshall was responsible for developing contemporary microeconomics, including the tools of supply and demand analysis. He explained how competitive markets cleared and why this was an optimal result," explains Steven Pressman, a professor of economics and finance at Monmouth University and author of the book *Fifty Major Economists*. "Even better, in competitive markets everyone pays the same market-clearing price, although almost everyone who buys the good would be willing to pay a little bit more. The difference between these two figures is the consumer surplus; it is an extra benefit that goes to consumers in competitive markets."

In Marshall's view, the consumer surplus and the producer surplus are the welfare that both parties derive from engaging in economic behavior, a shared benefit that underpins our market economy. Marshall is considered one of a handful of truly great economists who profoundly shaped economic theory, and he also established economics as a separate subject. His notion of the consumer surplus is central to our understanding of how we benefit from economic transactions in our market economy.

Every day, sellers around the nation essentially make guesses about how much consumers will pay for a particular product or service. Marketing and research help refine those guesses greatly. But historically,

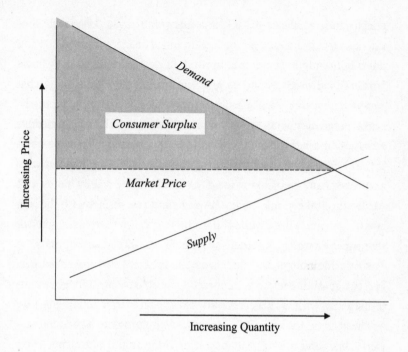

it's been very challenging for a producer to know what each individual would willingly pay, especially if a seller deals with thousands
of faceless customers. In that case, sellers pick an average price—
the highest they think the majority of their customers would be willing to pay. And by charging an average price, consumers willing to
pay more benefit. That means both consumers and producers share
the surplus.

But businesses that really know their customers extract the consumer surplus more effectively. Remember, that's how Bruce Nevins
got started selling water. He studied consumer focus groups to figure
out what consumers might pay for. You can see the principal at work
when a local plumber arrives to repair a leaking pipe in different
neighborhoods. The plumber works for himself, with the discretion to
charge what he likes, and when he arrives at a house in an upscale

Long Island neighborhood, he can see the grand house, the housekeeper who answers the door, and the fine antiques inside. When presenting the bill, he might double the normal charge because he knows the family can afford it. He might also know the family is throwing a big party that evening and needs the plumbing fixed immediately to avoid embarrassment. Next, the plumber might drive to a working-class neighborhood. There, he finds a young mother with three small children in a tiny house near the railroad tracks. Her one-and-only bathroom has been leaking for days now, and she finally had to call someone to take a look. When the plumber presents her with the bill, he charges her a little bit less than he might in other cases, sensing that times are tough and that she probably doesn't have the funds.

As the plumber goes about his day, he thinks about every customer and the amount each would be willing or able to pay. It happens automatically, without his even really trying. Most individual sellers do it. Think about car mechanics or anyone who provides a personal service. They tend to size you up first in order to judge how much you might be willing to pay. And it might not even be in the form of the final price but to set expectations for a tip. A hairdresser, for instance, might go out of her way to flatter or chat up a wealthy customer with the expectation that a good tip will result. The principle is universal. When a business really knows its customers, it possesses valuable information that helps it charge not what the impersonal market will bear but what each individual customer will bear.

If every purchase in the economy were individually negotiated, then either the producer or the consumer would take more of the surplus. For a small business where everyone knows each other, that might be possible. For a big business, until now, that simply has not been practical. It has been far more efficient to sell huge volumes at uniform prices than to pay clerks to haggle with customers over pennies. But what happens in the economy when a seller does capture more of the consumer surplus? That might leave consumers with less money to spend on other goods, essentially lowering the demand for such goods and reducing the consumer surplus in other markets. If a company captures a really big amount of consumer surplus, it won't just impoverish consumers; it will put pressure on other companies as well.

The consumer surplus is an abstract idea, but it has concrete meaning for every person. It's tied up in everything we do, every time we pay (or don't pay) for everything we buy or enjoy. Every day, we buy lots of small things: a cup of coffee, lunch, a pair of shoes, or a birthday card. Less frequently, we make big purchases: a car, a home, or an education. Whenever we buy something, we pay less than the maximum we would willingly pay, and we keep the benefit. We can keep that extra money and do whatever we like with it: save it, spend it, or give it away. The more surplus a seller extracts, the higher the price we pay.

Now think about what happens if a seller knows you really need or want something. Take something we do frequently, say, buying gasoline. Imagine you're driving when suddenly you notice the gas tank is on empty. You pull into the nearest gas station without even looking at how much it's charging for regular gas. You're in a hurry to get to your next meeting. Plus, you know the station frequently gives discounts. As you swipe your credit card and key in your zip code for verification, a sign flashes across the screen: Sorry, no discount today, regular unleaded $5 a gallon. "Ouch," you think. You haven't paid that much for gas in a while. You crane your neck to look at the advertised price out front. Regular unleaded is $3.50 a gallon after discounts to "select customers." You wonder why you're paying almost $1.50 more a gallon. But what can you do? You're late now and with little time to waste. You could just get half a tank and fill it up later, but you don't need the added stress. So you fill the tank and drive away.

If sellers have the ability to know your particular situation, they can capture a chunk of consumer surplus at the moment you really want a product by making you pay more. Everyone is vulnerable to a knowledgeable seller. But the wealthy risk far more because they have more resources to call on. The consumer surplus for the wealthy then tends to be far larger than for those lower down in the pecking order, a point brought home in a recent account of a wealthy American family. When millionaire "General" Robert Wood Johnson Jr. lay dying of cancer at age seventy-four, he summed up the consumer surplus in a single sentence, saying, "I have millions and I would give everything I have if someone could make me well." All of us, at some point in our lives, will reach the point where we would give everything for what we want. We will want something so badly that we would pay all that we have in order to get it, whether it is an artificial kidney, a bottle of water, or a tank of gas. The richer we are, the greater the gain to the seller; generally speaking, the more we have, the more we are willing to pay.

The consumer surplus is the ultimate prize in the economy. What's at stake is vast—essentially your bank account, your home, and everything you own. But even that's not all. Your future earnings potential is at stake as well. In a major purchase such as college, a car, or a home, prices can be based on expected income. Home mortgages, for example, let consumers pay even more than what they actually have for a house. And earning potential is the key factor in getting a mortgage. The more a bank expects you to earn in the future, the more it is willing to lend and the higher the price you can afford to pay. So what's at stake when the consumer surplus is up for grabs? It's not just everything you have ever earned. It's what you may earn in the future too. In the past, no company or seller has possessed the tools to extract large portions of consumer surplus systematically and with precision. Until now.

2

The Disappearing Mass Market

n 1921 the Ford Motor Company seemed unbeatable. With a market share almost five times the size of General Motors' (GM), Ford dominated the car market. No one even came close. While Ford accounted for 56 percent of passenger cars produced in the United States, GM, Ford's nearest competitor, only accounted for 12 percent. Alfred Sloan, GM's vice president, knew the numbers only too well. A few years earlier, he had devised a plan to revitalize GM, but the previous president, GM founder William Durant, wouldn't hear of it. Now Sloan had an ally, Pierre DuPont, GM's newly appointed president.

It was obvious to Sloan that GM could not compete with Ford on price. Henry Ford was the ultimate cost cutter. By producing cars on a large scale, efficiently and with no frills, Ford had created an automobile for the masses. Prior to Ford's brilliant innovation and insight, cars remained toys for the very wealthy. But Ford envisioned a car for everyone, and that meant a price everyone could afford. When Ford first launched his Model T in 1908, the price was $825. By 1915 he cut the price to $400, and by 1925 the price would be lower still at $275.

Ford was able to cut the price of his Model T because he made a standard product. The Model T was at the cutting edge, technologically, when first introduced, but its design was simple and that meant the automobile was easy to assemble. Over time, Ford abandoned plans for several other models, instead focusing solely on the Model T and making production evermore efficient. Ford famously offered his customers a Model T in any color they wanted, as long as it was black. He used the quickest and least expensive method of painting cars. And the rewards of producing a standard product were immense. At the height of Ford's popularity, half the cars in the world were Model Ts.

Sloan sensed an opportunity in Ford's focus on the mass market and found the crack he needed to exploit. GM couldn't offer cheaper cars. But GM would offer something Ford wouldn't: a wider variety of cars and the choice to customize the product. In Sloan's view, fundamental innovation was too expensive, but cosmetic innovation was cheap, fast, and thrilling for customers. Sloan relied on small changes to alter the looks of otherwise standard models and set out to capture Ford's market. GM created five distinct brands—Chevrolet, Pontiac, Oldsmobile, Buick, and Cadillac—segmenting the market into pricing tiers that looked distinctive but in fact were based on little more than cosmetic differences. In contrast to Ford's single product, GM would sell "a car for every purse and purpose." Sometimes various GM brands shared the same basic body shell, but the company attached different fenders, taillights, headlights, and trim to make the cars distinct. Black was boring so GM developed a new lacquer paint called Duco that allowed customers to pick a car of almost any color. Sloan went even further, unveiling a new model of car every year to excite customers. The new models, although not much different from an engineer's perspective, were entirely new to consumers' eyes.

The results were stunning. In just four years, GM's market share rose to 20 percent while Ford's market share dropped to 40 percent. By 1927 GM outsold Ford, and Ford's sales began to plummet. Ford stopped producing the Model T and unveiled the Model A, which looked more luxurious. Two years later Ford's market share was 31 percent and GM's market share was 32 percent. In 1940 GM dominated the global market with a 48 percent market share; Ford's market share was 19 percent. As market shares diverged, so did profitability. Ford suffered big losses during the 1930s while GM made sizeable profits. The two companies had completely reversed positions.

The rise of GM and the fall of Ford in the 1920s marked the beginning of the end for the consumer mass market. Ford created the epitome of a standard product, an identical Model T for every customer. Sloan's genius was in understanding that Americans wanted cars to be distinctive and sought to distinguish themselves through their choice of automobile. Customers who at first were thrilled with a Model T soon wanted more. Doctors and corporate executives didn't want to be seen driving the same car as ordinary blue-collar workers. Sloan catered to this new and growing demand for distinction and choice. When Ford created the Model T and drove prices down to $275 a car, he left a lot of consumer surplus on the table—money that consumers would have spent but that stayed in their pockets. With some simple customizing, GM was able to capture an additional chunk of the consumer surplus. Small changes, even as simple as offering a bright-red car instead of a black car, allowed GM to charge higher prices than the standard black Model T and sell more cars than Ford. GM's spectacular success began a trend away from single, standard products toward the increasing market segmentation and product customization that continues today.

Coffee Beans: From Mass Market to Niche Product

Mass markets have always been changing. Ever since the emergence of the mass market, companies like GM have sought to divide markets into segments on the basis of consumer affluence and taste. The trend accelerated during the twentieth century as the number of product choices available to consumers proliferated rapidly. As markets broke down into smaller and smaller segments, the effects were profound and the changes were very real for consumers. For example, take a simple agricultural product like coffee. In the 1950s a "cup of coffee" was a standard item across the country. Today, there's no such thing. And that has big implications for consumers and markets. When new coffee products entered the market, choices expanded, but less benign effects also came into play.

If one could pinpoint the moment in time when the coffee market began to change, it may have been the introduction of an ultraluxury coffee called *kopi luwak*. Today, kopi luwak is just about the most expensive coffee imaginable, a product sold at lavish stores like Harrods in London. This coffee bean, harvested from plantations in Indonesia, was discovered and introduced to Great Britain in the 1990s by Tony Wild, a director of coffee at Taylor's of Harrogate, the tea-and-coffee emporium owned by his family in the North of England.

Wild remembers the moment it all began. He was trying to get off the phone after talking to a coffee trader from Switzerland for the past hour and was getting fed up. The trader was flogging the same old premium coffee—Kenyan, Costa Rican, and Colombian, all the usual suspects. But Wild was looking for a way to put his family's business on the map. He wanted something that stood out from the crowd, something exotic. Ultimately, he wanted something that coffee aficionados would pay up for. Coffee and tea were in Wild's blood. His great uncle had come over to England after World War I from Switzerland and opened up a string of elegant cafés known as Betty's in the idyllic spa town of Harrogate and other locations in the North of England. Wild's father took over Betty's and merged it with Taylor's of Harrogate in the 1960s, and when Wild was old enough, he was sent to London to learn everything he could about coffee.

As he listened impatiently that day to the coffee trader, a vague recollection of something Wild had read years earlier came into his mind. During Wild's apprenticeship, he had spent many hours in the International Coffee Organization Library, in the center of London. On one occasion as he was flicking through an issue of *National Geographic* something caught his eye, a small article on a very unusual tasting and extremely rare coffee from the Indonesian island of Sumatra. "What was it called again?" he wondered. Kopi something. It had to be. *Kopi* meant "coffee" in Indonesian. And then he had it. "Listen," he interrupted the trader, "find me a kilo of Kopi Luwak and I'll buy it from you." The trader agreed, eager to make a sale, and with that the call ended. Wild soon forgot all about kopi luwak, never really expecting the trader to follow through.

Three months after Wild's initial request for kopi luwak, he got a call from the Swiss trader. "I have your kilo of Kopi Luwak," he said. Wild was surprised. "Oh right," he said. "How much?" "$150," said the trader, about fifty times the prevailing price of arabica at the time. As they made arrangements, Wild began thinking about what to do with his unusual find.

Wild loved a good story, and he thought the story of kopi luwak was about as good as they came. *Luwak* is the Indonesian word for "Asian palm civet," a small catlike creature found in the island jungles. So *kopi luwak* meant "civet coffee." Wild thought people would find civet coffee fascinating because of the unusual way the beans were processed. Wild civets wandered onto plantations to nibble the coffee berries. After twenty-four hours or so in their digestive tract, the coffee berries were excreted intact and then collected and washed for production. According to coffee experts, the time the coffee berries spend in the digestive tract alters the coffee's flavor. The fact that this process occurs on isolated plantations, almost like a freak of nature, means the supply of kopi luwak is limited.

Assembling a group of journalists at Taylor's a few weeks later, Wild prepared various coffees to sample. When it came time for the group to try kopi luwak, he told them the story of its production. It intrigued the dozen or so journalists present, leading to a lively and energetic discussion. In the months that followed, Wild became the go-to expert on coffee. "Kopi Luwak was my greatest triumph," Wild says today. "It led to our business becoming a national business."

The introduction of kopi luwak also led to big changes in the coffee industry and launched the ultraluxury coffee market. Prior to kopi luwak, there were three main segments of the coffee market: low end, middle, and premium. Each category consisted of millions of consumers. But kopi luwak changed that. Wild, in fact, not only launched a new product but created a new segment of the premium coffee market, the ultraluxury coffee market. It wasn't until years later that Wild discovered what he had done. A few years after his kopi luwak discovery, Wild left the family business to pursue his literary ambitions. He wrote a book in 2002 called *Coffee: A Dark History*. Over the following decade, Wild hadn't paid too much attention to the coffee business—until he had to delve into it again for the sake of updating his book. It was 2012 and Wild found, to his amazement, that kopi luwak had become a sensation among the global elite. Harrods in London sold kopi luwak by the half kilo in fancy golden bags for about $700, a gift for the Russian oligarch who had everything. Oprah tasted kopi luwak on her show and described the flavor to her audience. And the film "The Bucket List" made a big point of mentioning the exotic coffee. By 2012 kopi luwak had gained a reputation as the most expensive and coveted coffee in the world. "My little protégé," Wild remembered thinking at the time. "Ain't she done well!"

As kopi luwak has grown in popularity, so has its production. In the wild, only about 1,000 pounds are produced worldwide each year. But demand for the exotic coffee has grown so great that farmed production is estimated to be closer to five hundred tons annually, a thousand times more than what is produced naturally. As this dawned on Wild, he began to feel uneasy about the impact on civets. When he read a piece in the *Guardian* about wild civets being caged and force-fed coffee beans to produce kopi luwak, he was horrified. "What originally appealed to me was that you had this cute furry animal coming onto a coffee plantation and nibbling the beans and going away and leaving the beans with an interesting flavor," he said. "It was very quirky, charming and faintly disgusting. Now it's turned into something absolutely cruel and vile and a shock." Since discovering the dark side of kopi luwak, Wild has sought ways to end the abuse of civets. He went undercover for a British Broadcasting Corporation (BBC) investigation into kopi luwak production. He petitioned Harrods until they stopped selling a brand that was not wild. And he launched a campaign in late 2013 to certify genuine kopi luwak and drive out the production of caged-civet coffee. In a twist of fate, Wild, who brought kopi luwak to the world, now campaigns against its mass production.

Kopi luwak symbolizes how much the coffee market has changed. In 1950 a cup of coffee in the United States was the same in New York City or in Kalamazoo, Michigan—a cup of regular percolator coffee with cream or sugar. Back then, American coffee represented the ultimate commodity: uniform, inexpensive, and frankly, not that great. But that meant everyone knew what they were getting when they ordered a cup of coffee. Most importantly though, everyone knew what they would pay for a cup of coffee: one dime, including refills.

Today, who even knows the price of a cup of coffee? In a single block in New York City's Greenwich Village, customers spend radically different amounts for a cup of coffee. A shot of kopi luwak at a specialty café will set you back $30, and a *venti* skim latte from Starbucks costs around $5 while a regular cup of coffee at a nearby Dunkin' Donuts costs $1.19. Many different factors affect the price of a cup of coffee today. Is it espresso or regular filter coffee, fair trade or organic, small or gigantic, served in a hotel or from a street cart? The market for coffee has fragmented, and coffee is sold in myriad forms. Coffee is approaching the intricacy and specialization of the wine industry as different climatic conditions, soil, and even neighboring foliage are carefully observed and then linked to product through marketing. It's no longer just "coffee" when every bean has its own story.

This is amazing when you stop to think that there are really only two basic varieties of coffee: arabica, which accounts for over 60 percent of world production, and robusta. Arabica beans are slightly larger than robusta beans and require slightly cooler and drier conditions to grow. But businesses, with the eager participation of consumers, have created many different market segments based on how the berries are grown to how the coffee is brewed and everything in between. Start with how the coffee berries are grown: Are they fair trade or organic? And different climate conditions create varied aromas. The International Coffee Organization tracks eighteen aromas, from animal-like to woody. Then there are different tastes and ways the coffee feels in one's mouth. Is the coffee roasted a certain way? Finally, it comes to brewing: espresso, drip, French press, stove top, percolator, single-cup machine, or instant? The choices seem endless. Within the espresso category alone, buyers may select among cappuccino, latte, mocha, flat white, Americano, macchiato, café au lait, cortado, ristretto, and doppio, and that doesn't even take into account the syrup-flavored coffee drinks or the iced and frozen varieties that are also popular. And finally, consider where the coffee is served. Does it arrive in fine china in an elegant and luxurious setting or in a paper cup passed over the cash tin?

In the United States, Starbucks was a major force behind the breakdown of the mass coffee market. As Starbucks cafés emerged in the late 1980s, Americans were able to buy varieties of coffee previously only available in fine restaurants or during trips to Italy or elsewhere in Europe. Americans loved the new options, the various espresso drinks, and the oddly named sizes, and Starbucks cafés multiplied across the country. Partly, it was a new daily ritual of going out for coffee, and partly, the coffee just tasted better than most Americans were accustomed to. The change, though, means higher prices. While a regular drip-filter coffee can cost one dollar for a cup, a small latte from Starbucks, or "tall" as the company calls it, is three times the price.

The coffee market in the United States continues to evolve with greater segmentation. Now Americans pay a premium for customized, painstakingly prepared coffees. At Gregory's Coffee in New York City, baristas prepare individual coffees tailored to customer preferences. Whether you want lighter roasts or fresher coffee beans harvested more recently, the person preparing your coffee will make it carefully to your requirements. Perhaps you want the Australian version of café au lait known as a flat white? No problem. And what do you mean by milk? Whole, skim, organic, soy, almond, coconut—and the list goes on. And then some specialty coffee shops roast their own beans and seek out new coffees from around the world. As Starbucks becomes associated with the '80s and '90s, these specialty cafés are beginning to take over locations from Starbucks as the company that once revolutionized coffee is passed by another iteration of the market.

All that choice is having an interesting effect on our consumption of coffee. Between the 1950s and the 1970s, coffee consumption declined, according to the National Coffee Association of America. Since the 1980s, coffee consumption in the United States has increased and is almost back to where it was at its peak. Although the consumption of instant coffee, decaf, and traditional gourmet has declined, the consumption of frozen coffee drinks and lattes has risen. That means specialty coffee shops are booming. According to figures from the *New York Times*, in 2014 a coffee shop opened every three days in New York City, and the high-end customized cafés seemed to be expanding.

Meanwhile, the American coffee drinker spends more money on coffee than ever before. Partly that has to do with the price of coffee beans rising in response to drought and climate change. But partly it has to do with the multitude of choice involved in ordering a cup of coffee. The variety of coffee drinks has ballooned but so have the prices. Surveys find that on average each American worker spends $1,092 a year on coffee, or $4 for every workday. And that kind of money surprises many of us who don't expect a daily coffee to add up to a big-ticket item. Even accounting for inflation, spending by American workers on coffee in the 1950s didn't come close.

As the market for coffee has changed we have more choice, and we get better value, but we also pay more for every cup. We know a customized cappuccino with specially roasted beans from an exotic part of the world is likely to be more expensive than a regular filter coffee from a truck, but we don't know how much more. Try searching for what an average cup of coffee costs, and it's quite challenging to find an authoritative source. According to the website Statistic Brain, the average price of a brewed coffee is $1.38, while the average price of an espresso drink is closer to $2.45. But is that in New York City where rents and other costs are high? Or in a small town where rents and costs would be lower? It's not easy locating good price information on products or knowing if it's already out of date. Often, searching the web for prices means trolling through chat sites and piecing together advertisements. Who's even compiling price information these days that can be readily accessed by consumers? It's not as if there's a consumer reports shopping comparison for coffee. In fact, the only reliable sources on prices are the companies themselves. They have all that valuable price information at their fingertips, but they're not sharing it with consumers.

As the market for coffee has broken down into many different components, we have no reliable way of knowing if we're paying a fair price for what we're getting. As the standard cup of filter-drip coffee disappeared, so too did our understanding and knowledge of what a cup of coffee should cost. Starbucks imposed a new standard for espresso drinks, but as that breaks down and coffee chains introduce "painstakingly prepared coffees, made to order," as the *New York Times* reported in its Dining section in May 2014, a standard cup of coffee will cease to exist and so will standard pricing. And although the high end has driven coffee innovation, the idea that coffee can cost five dollars or more has benefited low-end coffee sellers. Dunkin' Donuts doesn't publish its business details because it's a private company owned, since 2008, by three major private equity firms: Bain, Carlyle, and Thomas H. Lee. It's a safe bet, though, that those savvy investors recognized that when Starbucks taught people that coffee could be worth five dollars a cup, it created an opportunity to raise prices on more mundane coffee products.

The Splintering of the Mass Market

Major economic shifts take time to play out, and the breakdown of the mass market is no different. As with most significant changes, the result for consumers has been mixed. Mass markets have brought many benefits to both consumers and producers. As a relatively recent phenomenon, mass markets came into their own in the twentieth century as businesses offered uniform goods at uniform prices to huge populations. In order to promote the mass purchase of goods, methods of mass communication blanketed the landscape. First newspapers, then radio, and finally television broadcast consistent messages to the public. In order to move vast quantities of product, haggling was banned in favor of transparent pricing. Marketing executives aimed their efforts at their largest opportunity, the "average" consumer. The benefits were huge: material abundance, affordable prices, and substantial profits.

The establishment of transparent markets with uniform prices allowed companies to profit as never before. When a seller produces a product for less than the market price, the seller earns a surplus of its own. In the mass-market era, producers achieving the lowest cost and offering the most desirable goods captured huge sales and stacked up unprecedented fortunes. American consumer icons ruled the markets: first Ford, then Coke, Tide, and Budweiser. Companies made products to benefit the consumer, reducing the effort spent on household chores, lowering cost, and improving quality and reliability when compared to locally produced goods. Profits piled up at mighty American corporations and flowed through to stockholders.

For consumers, the benefits of mass markets were even greater. Ordinary consumers enjoyed a growing range of choices and, collectively, the power to choose winners and losers in the economy. Mass markets defined an era of consumer "sovereignty" in which the market, consisting of the individual decisions of millions of shoppers, told companies what items to make and how many to deliver. Companies studied consumer habits and guessed at what they could offer busy households next to make chores easier and more efficient. Throughout the era of the mass market, the American consumer economy boomed, and a lot of surplus remained with consumers rather than going to producers. That fostered a degree of affluence never before seen in American history. As consumers had more money to spend, they did so, driving economic growth into the second half of the twentieth century. The development of mass markets fundamentally enabled the existence of an affluent middle class alongside a successful corporate sector in the United States. For years the mass markets provided a measure of stability to both producers and consumers.

The evolution of the coffee market followed a recognized pattern. In many ways it paralleled the evolution of the bottled-water market. Prior to Perrier, most Americans drank tap water and paid a low price. But Bruce Nevins took a generic product like water and separated it into two markets: bottle and tap. Tap was the low-cost alternative and bottled water occupied the middle-to-luxury market. Then within the bottled market, more segments were created. Dasani and Aquafina entered the fray, capturing the market for bottled water in the middle range. Evian and Pellegrino served the high end. And since then, many more high-end waters have entered the market. Consumers can buy

"Tasmanian Rainwater," glacial water named "10 Thousand BC," and even "Kona Nigari," water distilled from the deep ocean off the coast of Hawaii and sold in a concentrated form. In a Milan department store, a shiny gold bottle of "Bling" water will set you back 350 euros, more than $400. In water, coffee, and many other markets, segmentation has increased, and average prices have risen.

As we move away from standardized products and services, companies that once rode the wave of mass markets are now slicing and dicing the mass market into smaller and smaller segments to differentiate prices and capture more of the consumer surplus. Think about it this way: Try to imagine a product that all Americans consume today, whether high income, low income, or superrich. There was a time when most households had a Model T Ford parked on the property (even if they also had a Rolls) or a Hoover vacuum cleaner in the closet. Kitchen pantries in every kind of neighborhood stocked cans of Campbell's soup and bottles of Heinz ketchup. Today perhaps the best remaining example of a truly mass-market product may be Coca-Cola. Warren Buffet drinks the same Coke that everyone else does. So far, Coca-Cola hasn't created different market segments for Coke according to the means of consumers. Coca-Cola has varied its offerings with new flavors and ingredients, but so far only in a limited range. Diet Coke and regular Coke typically cost the same. You can pay more for Coke in the iconic glass bottle or for Coke from Mexico made with cane sugar instead of corn syrup, but there's no true luxury Coke, nor is there a low-end Coke. For the most part, it's a standard product for the entire U.S. market. But elsewhere in the economy, the proliferation of various types of one product, according to how much a consumer is willing to pay, is the norm. Think of toothpastes, with their many different flavors, different colors, and different reasons for use. One whitens, one fights cavities, one freshens breath best, and another protects enamel. Colgate alone produces some two dozen different varieties of toothpaste, and that doesn't include brands for children. Or think of other products like canned pasta sauces. Ragu alone has about thirty-six different varieties, often with different price points.

The growing segmentation of markets is sold as a benefit, and of course it does provide benefits. But it also obscures price. Consumers have many more choices but correspondingly less certainty about whether a given price is fair. How much more is Fiji water worth compared to Poland Spring? The only information consumers have is what's listed on the shelf. Sellers possess all the information about what the differences really are and how much it costs to make each product. Consumers have almost none. Think back to coffee. A coffee at Dunkin' Donuts costs around one dollar while a coffee at Starbucks costs around four dollars. Which is a better deal for the consumer? How much profit is in each?

Considerable evidence shows that market segmentation yields prices that are not tied directly to costs. Perhaps that should be obvious because if there weren't profit in it we wouldn't see so much segmentation. The Australian flagship airline Qantas flies daily from Los Angeles to Sydney, a trip that takes roughly fourteen hours to complete. On those long-haul flights, comfort is important, but upon looking at the different price points, you wonder whether Qantas's pricing reasonably reflects its costs. A round-trip flight in economy class can cost $2,000 while the same flight in first class costs $15,000 for a trip booked in December 2014. Does a first-class seat really cost Qantas almost eight times that of an economy seat? There's more room— around the equivalent of five premium economy seats—better food, and of course less time waiting in line to check in. But there's also less passenger and luggage weight, which means the plane can use less fuel or carry more paid cargo. Airline experts confirm that premium seating is more profitable than economy seating. It all points to companies' greater abilities to extract additional surplus from consumers by segmenting the market, particularly at the high end.

As companies slice and dice up markets into finer and finer segments, the number of consumers in each market shrinks and so does the power held by the sheer number of consumers in mass markets. Think back to coffee and the millions of consumers in each segment of the market: low, middle, and premium. Today the market for kopi luwak may be in the thousands. As the trend of market segmentation progresses to its logical conclusion, the number of consumers in a given segment drops until finally only one single consumer exists for a given product. With that shift in numbers comes a shift in power. One consumer has no leverage against a mighty company.

It's a dramatic reversal from the days of the mass market, when there was power in numbers. Getting a million consumers to buy your product is a very different equation from getting one consumer you know very well to buy it. Think of potato chips, for example. A potato-chip maker wants to sell to a million people. One-third of those people just want potato chips and are not fussy about flavor or price. They're in a hurry and will take what they can get. The next third are willing to pay up but only if the chips taste good and are of excellent quality. The last third of customers don't care so much about taste but will not pay more than two dollars for a party-sized bag of chips. If the potato-chip manufacturer could pick these groups off one by one, it could offer the first group inferior-quality potato chips for three dollars and the second group better chips for the same price. The third group could get inferior chips discounted to two dollars. None of that is possible if the seller can't separate the market into segments. If the seller doesn't know who is who and wants to capture the entire one million, it must sell high-quality potato chips to everybody but priced at two dollars a bag. In that case all three groups of consumers fare better than if they had been segmented into separate groups, and the producer has to forego those additional profits. However, if the seller slices up the market into those three groups, the seller gets more of the surplus, leaving the consumers worse off.

Meanwhile, as market segmentation marches on, the quality of information available to consumers drops. If fifty laundry detergents are on offer, each with different ingredients and different prices, it is no easy thing for consumers to pick the best for them. Consumer confusion rising from the multitude of available choices is an area ripe for exploitation. Selling brands that a consumer trusts and buys out of habit, even if they aren't the most economical or the most suitable, is a profitable business.

There's another aspect to growing market segmentation. As markets become more segmented, public goods become less valued. For instance, if everyone drinks their own brand of bottled water, they care less about the quality of the local water supply. As more people install electricity-producing generators, they care less about the reliability of the public grid. Dividing consumers into smaller and smaller groups means they do not share common interests and don't make collective demands. It's an effective way of reducing consumer power and driving down the demand for shared goods. For another example, take public education. When more and more wealthy Americans send their children to private school, fewer people willingly invest in quality public education. Market segmentation reinforces social inequality and our notions of difference. As markets splinter, consumers are not all in the same boat.

To be sure, the breakdown of mass markets isn't all bad. Product differentiation is about giving consumers more choices, after all, and choice is an important component of wealth. And we have certainly seen the value of products and services increase. You'd be hard pressed to find anyone who doesn't believe that coffee tastes better in the United States today than it did in the 1950s. Today, consumers can find any type of coffee they desire in virtually any part of the country. The segmentation of the market holds the promise of satisfying every whim, every dream. But there's a cost. Water is more expensive in a bottle. For that price, you're getting a bottle, convenience, and perhaps the mental image of a far-off paradise. Coffee is more expensive when customized according to type of beans, how it is roasted, how it is brewed, and how it is served—not to mention the beautiful patterns, like works of art, on the milk froth of a latte. These days baristas even hold competitions over the best frothy pictures!

Today we're so focused on choice, we're not thinking about what we're giving up. As the mass market disappears, so does the standard price and our ability to see what others are paying for the same product. And it's happening everywhere in the economy, from coffee to financial services.

Think about banking for a moment. Do you know the interest rate of a thirty-year mortgage today? If you are a homeowner, you may have a rough idea. But you can only have a rough idea because every bank offers different terms and treats every borrower individually. Not long ago banks posted their mortgage rates, and either you qualified or you didn't. Home buyers had a pretty good idea of what a thirty-year mortgage was going to cost. That's not the case today: There's no longer a standard thirty-year mortgage offered. Pricing depends on the terms of the loan and the strength of the borrower's credit. The worse your credit, the more you pay. That's logical from the banks' perspective because they believe bad credit means higher risk. But it's perverse from the borrower's perspective because it means that those with the fewest options and least wherewithal will pay the most. Most importantly, from the consumer's point of view, how do you know if you're getting a fair deal?

Think about this effect elsewhere in the economy. You used to be able to go into just about any McDonald's and order a cheeseburger at a standard cost. Not anymore. McDonald's restaurants have different pricing and different product bundling. When you look on the McDonald's website, they provide plenty of information about the nutrition and calories of each burger, sandwich, or product. But nothing is stated about the price. There's no way to know what you'll pay for a cheeseburger in a McDonald's in Santa Barbara, California, or San Antonio, Texas. And there's no good source, online or elsewhere, to find out.

Wherever you look, it becomes increasingly apparent that we're more and more in the dark when it comes to prices. Monthly cellphone charges are notoriously difficult to understand and seem to change from month to month inexplicably. How do you find out what a fair price is for cell-phone service? No one can even begin to answer that question. But it's critical to know whether consumers are getting a fair deal. In the United States, for instance, where cell phones are increasingly overtaking landlines, no one has an up-to-date study of how prices compare with other countries. Most people probably have a sense that their cell-phone service is too high, but until there are hard numbers, it's hard for any changes to occur. The last detailed study was published by the Open Technology Institute, part of the New America Foundation, a think tank based in New York and Washington, DC. In this 2010 study, the Open Technology Institute found that the minimum cost of a complete cell-phone package in the United States was $59.99 a month compared with $32.40 a month in the United Kingdom. So prices in the United Kingdom tend to be half that of the United States. Without meaningful price comparisons, it's impossible for consumers to demand lower prices. A director of the Open Technology Institute, Sascha Meinrath, says that means over the next decade, U.S. consumers could overpay by over a quarter-of-a-trillion dollars for worse levels of service than customers in other countries. It's also interesting to note the reason the Open Technology Institute hasn't updated its study. "The best numbers I've seen are the ones that we dug up ourselves," says Meinrath, "which required putting multilingual staff onto this project full time for quite some time to talk with providers in each of those countries and find out what a consumer plan actually costs—this is probably why no one's done this sort of analysis since." Cell-phone pricing is terribly opaque and requires enormous financial and human resources to make it accessible to consumers. What hope does one consumer alone have to know whether he or she is getting a fair deal?

It's not just cell phones, of course. Think about the market for health care. Thanks to Obamacare, we have a little bit more visibility on how much the cost of health insurance is each year, but try understanding what it costs to visit the doctor or have any kind of procedure done. No one, not even the hospitals or doctor's office, can answer that question. It's an impossibly complicated system of different co-pays, different coverages, and different deductibles. And that's if you have health insurance. If you don't, the doctor's office can charge whatever it wants. Need a knee or hip replacement and live in the New York region? The average price of a knee or hip replacement at St. Joseph's Medical Center in Yonkers, New York, is $17,068, while at Christ Hospital in Jersey City, the average cost is $139,072. Both are large general medical and surgical hospitals in the New York City area, some thirty miles apart in fact, yet one charges eight times as much as the other for the same basic procedure.

There's virtually no area of the economy left where we all know what something costs. Milk? Every grocery store charges its own price and runs its own promotions. And is the milk organic, hormone-free, or just basic? How about a car? It depends on the options. College? That depends on your income and assets. Price is the most important signal for consumers in the marketplace. It's the way you make decisions. It's the number at which a product or service trades at, and therefore it encapsulates everything in a single point. Without open and transparent pricing, uniform products, and orderly markets, sellers can spread a thick fog over consumers while maintaining crystal-clear vision themselves. If you can't see what others are paying and getting, how do you know you're getting a fair deal? But sellers hold all the cards. They know exactly what you and everyone else pays, plus they know how much it costs them to make.

Mass markets are breaking down because it's more profitable for sellers to create finer and finer market segments. Sellers see an opportunity to divide the market into smaller fragments in which they can charge various different prices instead of one average price. By dividing up the market into smaller groups, sellers can make better guesses at the maximum price consumers in each group would be willing to pay. Small differences in products can allow sellers to charge big differences in prices. So what does the disappearing mass market mean? It means that sellers are gaining more of the consumer surplus. And that trend has been going on for several decades now.

In theory, the splintering of mass markets can provide greater choice and create wealth for consumers and sellers alike. And perhaps that would be the result if many sellers competed for our business. But in practice breaking the market into ever-smaller segments turns out to be a convenient way to gobble up consumer surplus and exploit the vulnerable. It's no coincidence companies try to atomize markets because that lets them charge more to those who will pay more. The breakdown of the mass market obscures the general price level and obfuscates the market power behind a seeming plethora of products. Without a mass market it is difficult, and often impossible, for consumers to see whether they are paying a fair price.

The Internet was supposed to empower consumers with knowledge. On a smartphone, consumers stepping into a store should immediately be able to see what other stores charge for the same product. That would be true if we were all buying the exact same product. But growing production differentiation means there is no average or standard product, and there's no average or standard price. Even in the era of data and the Internet, the prices we pay for everything from cars to coffee to college have become less transparent, not more. Companies have all the knowledge in terms of price. They know how much it costs to make their products, and they have the resources to know what the competition is charging. Consumers, on the other hand, have little knowledge of price. They have no idea what it costs to produce the products, they have few resources to compare prices across the economy, and they have no idea at what minimum price the companies would sell the products. With big data and analytics, companies are further increasing the knowledge gap, and that means the power dynamics in the marketplace are shifting again. Four centuries ago, the English philosopher Francis Bacon said knowledge is power. And that's especially true when it comes to the economy in the digital age.

3

The Knowledge Gap

On Friday, April 4, 2014, Google added a few sentences to its terms of service agreement displayed on its website. For the most part, the change in policy was a nonevent, prompting few if any headlines. But it finally confirmed something many had suspected: If you use Gmail, Google reads your messages.

That shocking admission produced very little in the way of public reaction—which is surprising because the security and the privacy of written communication have long been basic legal principles in the United States and in Europe. Concerns about intercepting and reading mail date back to the beginnings of postal service: In the 1630s, under the reign of Louis XIII of France, the brilliant-but-authoritarian Cardinal Richelieu established the *cabinet noir*, a "black room" where mail was opened and read prior to delivery. Such snooping has never been popular, and today the security of the mail is written into the constitutions of several European countries.

Prior to Google's admission, there had been plenty of speculation about whether the Internet giant read e-mail correspondence. Some even went so far as to devise a test. In early 2013 High-Tech Bridge, a cybersecurity company, tested fifty Internet companies to see whether any read their customers' e-mails. The security firm set a clever trap. It used each company's system to send private e-mail that contained a unique web address. The techies at High-Tech Bridge then watched to see if any of the companies visited the website. Over the course of the ten-day experiment, several companies clicked on the link. Among them were Google, Facebook, and Twitter. So Google, Facebook, and Twitter were caught clicking on links supposedly only known to the sender and the receiver of the e-mail. At the time, a spokesperson at Google dismissed High-Tech Bridge's results as nothing new. Then later that year, in response to a lawsuit brought against Google, the Internet firm said Gmail users should not expect their e-mail to be private. After all, the implicit understanding is that because the Gmail service is free, the company is entitled to set the terms. But the implications of Google reading users' e-mails is a question that Gmail users have little hope of answering. Google won't say. And what about the users of other e-mail services who send e-mails to a Gmail address? Should they expect their e-mail correspondence to be read by Google too?

Consumers dominate the e-mail account market. Research group Radicati estimated the total number of e-mail accounts worldwide to be almost 4 billion in 2014. Out of that total, business e-mail accounts make up 25 percent while consumer accounts make up 75 percent. Radicati projects a strong increase in the number of consumer e-mail accounts due to the growth of online shopping because an e-mail address is required for any kind of e-commerce. In general, consumer e-mail makes money for providers through advertising. Companies study e-mail content to pitch the most relevant advertising to users. That's exactly what Google does.

Every time Google reads an e-mail, it garners personal information—clues about your finances, health, relationships, preferences, and tastes that can be used to sell you products. Because Google makes billions of dollars a year, it's a good bet that studying e-mail presents a very valuable opportunity for advertisers. And that opportunity is growing. In recent years the number of Gmail users has exploded. Today Gmail leads all other e-mail providers, including

Microsoft, Yahoo, and America Online. According to comSource, a company that reports on Internet use, global Gmail users fifteen years of age and older have grown more than fourfold since 2009, from 91.6 million to around 400 million today. Launched ten years ago, Gmail first became available to all comers in 2007. Google announced it had 425 million Gmail users in 2012 but has not updated the figure publicly. To be sure, Google knows its exact number of Gmail users, but when contacted, it only points to the 2012 figure. One can only speculate as to why Google won't provide up-to-date figures. Perhaps they would show that the company not only dominates search but dominates e-mail as well. About 12 billion Google searches are performed every month in the United States alone, and together with Gmail traffic and other services, Google appears to dominate the online world. No other company comes close to Google's user numbers. According to comScore, in August 2014 there were 12 billion Google searches conducted in the United States compared to the second-most popular search engine, Microsoft, with 3.5 billion searches, followed by 1.8 billion Yahoo searches. The scale of Google's data resource is unmatched, and it keeps growing every minute of every day.

For its part, Google has never tried very hard to clear up how it handles the contents of user e-mails and has even gone to some trouble to keep users in the dark. When a February 2014 court case involving Gmail and major media companies revealed details of its activities, Google asked the judge to redact information about its e-mail scanning process from a transcript of the public hearing. The judge ultimately did not allow the information to be redacted, and what came out of the court case was revealing. The court case exposed that in 2010, Google found itself unable to read millions of e-mails each day because users opened them up in Outlook or on their iPhones. Google devised a solution to catch its missing e-mail by changing the point at which it scanned e-mail messages. Instead of reading e-mail in the storage area of the transmission process, it moved scanning up to the point just before e-mail delivery. That means Google reads your e-mail before you do. And it also means that even if you don't read a message and delete it without opening it, Google will still review the contents. In the case, the plaintiffs explained it this way:

> Google made a choice. They said, you know what, when people are accessing emails by an iPhone, we are not able to get their information. When people aren't opening their emails or they are deleting them, we are not able to get their information. When people are using Google Apps accounts where ads are disabled, we are not able to get that information. When people are accessing Gmail through some other email provider, we are not able to get that information. So what they did is they took a device that was in existence already and operating just fine back in the storage area, and they moved it to the delivery pipeline.

In an opinion piece published in *USA Today*, lawyers who acted for the media companies in the Gmail court case pointed out the irony of Google's attempt to hide information about its e-mail reading: "Google's stated goal is to 'organize the world's information,' but they fought to avoid disclosing how and why they've done it. Now we know."

Although we might know a little more from the court case, Google rarely makes disclosures that it doesn't have to. Following the court case, Google had to clarify to users that it does read e-mail. And so it was that in April 2014, Google posted the following three lines on its website: "Our automated systems analyze your content (including emails) to provide you personally relevant product features, such as customized search results, tailored advertising, and spam and malware detection. This analysis occurs as the content is sent, received, and when it is stored." The first thing to notice is that Google states it reads Gmail with the help of an automated system. In the past

Google has made a point to say that no person actually reads your e-mail, as if that somehow should comfort users. But that's hardly reassuring. Google's automated system is far more efficient and thorough than mere humans could ever be. The automated system allows Google to scan every single e-mail, analyze it, and store it almost immediately. A person or even thousands of people trying to read and to catalog the e-mails of 400 million Gmail users every day wouldn't have a hope of accomplishing much.

Google, of course, maintains that what it does is good for you. By reading your e-mail, Google can provide you with personally relevant advertising and customize your Google searches. But what Google fails to explain is exactly how reading e-mail benefits Google. How much money does Google make from reading a given person's e-mail? Does all that "relevant" searching and advertising cost consumers something after all? What are the trade-offs?

Answers to those questions aren't easy to come by. As far as Google is concerned, information about Google is private. Google claims its activities can't be revealed for reasons of competition. And notice that Google doesn't make any promises about what it will do with all the information it collects. At the moment Google might even be doing some users a favor. But there's no restriction on what it may or may not do with all that data in the future. Finally, Google isn't just reading Gmail users' e-mails but any e-mail sent to a Gmail user or sent by a Gmail user. With 400 million Gmail users worldwide, Google has access to a lot of messages.

What Do We Know About Google?

We know that Google can read our e-mails. Wouldn't you like to read Google's e-mail? Imagine what Google CEO and cofounder Larry Page's e-mail would reveal. Wouldn't you like to know what he really thinks of Google users and what the company has in store for coming years? Of course that's not possible, unless you want to risk a lawsuit and possibly end up in jail. Google spends millions of dollars a year protecting its own privacy and guarding its secrets with care. Company lawyers craft nondisclosure and confidentiality agreements into all kinds of contracts to prohibit information about Google from being revealed publicly. So there's no doubt that Google treats its own information as private property and as something extremely valuable in the commercial world. And Google is not alone. Virtually all companies and organizations spend time and money protecting their privacy, whether through commercial services, nondisclosure agreements, or otherwise.

So how much money and effort do consumers spend to protect their privacy? Many people buy malware- or antivirus-detection software. But although that may help protect your computer from hackers and malicious programs, it does nothing to protect your privacy. Even individuals with substantial financial resources have few options for protecting individual privacy in the same way that companies do. The dichotomy between the privacy of firm information and the ready access to consumer information creates a huge knowledge gap. Companies can learn practically everything there is to know about us, but we possess only very limited information about them. What we do know is carefully orchestrated to portray a favorable image, whatever the reality may be.

Ask yourself: What do you know about Google? When you stop to think, you realize that you don't know all that much. Of course, there are places where you could find out more information. After all, it is a public company, so there are lots of sources. But when you look into it, the information Google is obliged to disclose reveals little. Google, like most public companies, carefully selects what information it releases publicly. Everything passes by its lawyers first. Even the company's senior executives must check with legal experts before they say anything.

Because Google is a public company, it must comply with Securities and Exchange Commission regulations of disclosure for public companies. That means it must file regular earnings reports, produce an annual report, and announce any material changes affecting its financial position. But if you've ever read an annual report, you know a company provides as little information about its business practices as it can get away with. Official filings are a highly crafted series of documents produced by accounting and legal experts both inside and outside the company. Google's annual report discloses the required facts about sales and earnings but also projects the image Google wants to present to the rest of the world—an image that has taken significant financial resources and manpower to create and protect.

Google's 2013 annual report spans some ninety-four pages and provides a basic description of what the company does in very general terms. In Google's case it earns money through advertising: 91 percent of revenues come from advertisers. The annual report provides an overview of its various business units and products, and highlights from the past financial year. It explains key elements critical to the business, for instance, research and development (R&D). Google spent $8 billion on R&D in 2013. The annual report also gives the reader a sense of the physical scale of the company: 48,000 full-time employees worldwide, with more than half of all revenues coming from outside the United States. It describes the threats to its business in general terms; possible threats from new technology, intense competition, legal suits, new regulations, and cyber attacks may affect its future earnings. Copies of the company's financial statements describe key financial indicators and break down costs and revenues, assets and liabilities, and reasons for any big variations from the previous year. Google's annual report is a static snapshot of the company. You might think of this report as an annual holiday card that you send out to your friends and relatives, providing a brief description of what happened during the year along with the best photo you can get.

Another resource is the company's website—again, a highly polished presentation of itself. When you visit the Google website, you find information similar to the company's annual report. You can also find news releases the company announces during the year. Google spends millions of dollars a year and lots of time and energy promoting its public image with a formidable staff of public-relations experts. Employees think long and hard about what information to release to the public and how to do that. The end result is that Google carefully and deliberately manages what you know about it.

Google guards its privacy very carefully. At the core of its business is Google's famous PageRank algorithm. That's the formula for determining why Google displays some sites and not others in response to a given search query and why it ranks certain pages higher than others. According to "Search Engines and Ethics" in the *Stanford Encyclopedia of Philosophy*, Google's algorithm contains 500 million variables and 2 billion terms, so it's not an easy thing to disclose in the first place. But nevertheless, it is the "secret sauce" that determines why Google's search differs from other search engines, and the company can keep that secret on the grounds of our intellectual property laws that protect a company from competitors. But keeping it secret has consequences for users. As the Stanford article on "Search Engines and Ethics" points out, "Concerns affecting objectivity and bias in the context of search engines are also closely related to controversies pertaining to the lack of 'openness' or 'transparency' . . . Because Google's PageRank algorithm is 'a patented and closely guarded piece of intellectual property' . . . we don't know the algorithm's formulas. And this factor, of course, makes it difficult to comment on an algorithm's objectivity or lack thereof." Because Google can keep its information secret, there's no way to know for sure if Google Search actually does what's best for users or if it exploits users in favor of Google's real customers, its advertisers. Or indeed in favor of Google itself.

Those who have studied Google from its beginning believe that as soon as Google sensed it was on to something lucrative it started to guard its privacy fiercely. In *The Search: How Google and Its Rivals Rewrote the Rules of Business and Transformed Our Culture*, author John Battelle describes how, in the early days, Google stopped revealing information about its business so that potential competitors would remain clueless about how profitable the market for search really was. "By the end of 2002, Google stopped publicly discussing its key internal metrics, claiming that it had more than 1,000 employees and more than 10,000 computers in its vaunted infrastructure," Battelle writes. "The company did still boast about the size of its web index, which passed 4 billion documents in December 2002. But it guarded its revenue numbers jealously—perhaps because they were so good: in 2002, the company made nearly $100 million on gross revenues of about $440 million. That's some serious cash, and the longer people like Bill Gates stayed in the dark about it, the longer Google could remain free from competition." Battelle sums up the double standards of the company this way: "As compared with Google the service, it has always been difficult to extract information from Google the company—clearly this was inherited from its founders, Page in particular."

Although Google doesn't want you to know much about Google, think about what it knows about you. If you use Google Search, Google knows your darkest, most intimate secrets and desires. Think about all the things you ask Google that you would never dare ask another person. Do I have a mood disorder? How can I make sex better with my spouse? Do I need to see a therapist? Google tracks everything you search and can distill a pretty detailed picture of your dreams, longings, struggles, and bad habits. Before you see your doctor, you are likely to google to find out what your symptoms could be. Cancer? Heart disease? If you are having trouble with your spouse, before you see an attorney, you're likely to google about divorce proceedings. Before you see your therapist, you may research antidepressants. Maybe you want to change jobs? Google knows before anyone else what job sites you've looked for. Google knows the most intimate details about each one of us and has the means to put together the pieces to paint a remarkably clear portrait. The fact that Google is still learning how to exploit what it has is small consolation to consumers. The increasing exploitation of private details by profit-seeking companies isn't a question of "if." It's only a matter of "when."

But Google doesn't just know our secrets. It also knows critical information about our location and what we are doing, which includes a detailed history of the facts of our life. Google can pinpoint us and track our every movement. Thanks to the "directions" service in Google Maps, Google often even knows where we will go next. Google knows our friends and family. It knows what groups we're involved with online. What we're reading, watching, and thinking about. And Google uses cookies to track our movements even on non-Google web pages. Imagine trying to do the same to Google. You would be charged with hacking and stand a good chance of ending up in jail. Although Google can't directly view your bank account online, it can put some very important pieces together and figure out your means. If you use Google's Wallet service, you actually link your bank account to Google, giving the company direct access to your bank account. When Google tracks your movements online, it can determine what bills you pay, what transactions you make, how healthy you are, and what you have in your financial accounts.

Google Search alone is a powerful way to gather user information, but add to that Google's ability to read and store your e-mail and everything you discuss online: your next family trip, your upcoming college reunion, or plans to sell your house. Plus, Google owns many other services that all gather, analyze, and store user data. Just some of these include Google Earth, Google Maps, YouTube, Blogger, Picasa, Orkut, Google Health, and Google Calendar. Not to mention Google's other products that gather our information offline like Google

Glass, the glasses that record everything the wearer sees, or a phone that watches and records everything you do. Google offers services to cover almost every aspect of our lives. And take into account that Google has three-quarters of the search market in the United States and more than 80 percent of the mobile search market, which means Google is already tracking the vast majority of Americans. In Europe, Google dominates completely with 90 percent of the search market. It's no wonder concern is growing among Europeans over Google's market power. With that kind of access, Google is quickly building individual portraits of millions of people that it can use for its own purposes. Perhaps at first the portraits lack clarity. But as the days, months, and years go by, the pictures sharpen.

Google already knows a lot about you, but it's not about to stop there. The company's ability to monitor you at every step of your day is tantalizingly close, and Google is aggressively expanding to cover every aspect of your life, both online and offline. In June 2014, at a conference for software developers in San Francisco, the company announced its plans to expand its products into your home and your car and even on your physical self. The conference helps software developers understand where Google is heading, so they can develop and provide the latest software for Google's new devices. Google's expansion into all areas offline is primarily through Android, its mobile operating system. The company has already launched Android Wear, in particular smartwatches that provide information such as traffic patterns, bus or train schedules, or package delivery. It's also working on an information system for the home as well as an information system for the car, Android Auto, which will pair with a smartphone. The main point emanating from the conference was that Google is clearly focusing on providing us devices that enable it to track us at every step of our lives, even at work. Google has also announced plans to push deeper into business computing with new e-mail systems, storage systems, and other services.

Knowing You Better Than You Know Yourself

In an interview with the *Guardian* in 2014, Ray Kurzweil, a well-known computer scientist, author, and futurist who is currently director of engineering at Google, explained what he is working on at Google, providing insight into the company's ambitions. Kurzweil's focus is to bring natural language understanding to Google. He explained it this way:

> My project is ultimately to base search on really understanding what the language means. When you write an article you're not creating an interesting collection of words. You have something to say and Google is devoted to intelligently organizing and processing the world's information. The message in your article is information, and the computers are not picking up on that. So we would like to actually have the computers read. We want them to read everything on the web and every page of every book, then be able to engage an intelligent dialogue with the user to be able to answer their questions.

The key to all this is scale. And Google has staggering scale. With access to billions of pages of information, Google can read, understand, and make connections between everything online. And that means that, as a practical matter, Google will know everything. As the *Guardian* explained in the article: "Google will know the answer to your question before you have asked it . . . It will have read every email you've ever written, every document, every idle thought you've ever tapped into a search-engine box. It will know you better than your intimate partner does. Better, perhaps, than even yourself."

It may take a few more years before Google actually knows you better than you know yourself, but it's no longer a question relegated to the world of science fiction. Google's relentless advance toward omniscience is only a matter of time. Indeed, Google already knows your most intimate personal details, things you would never want others to know. Yet you have no idea what Google is planning to do with all that knowledge and, perhaps even more importantly, what limits Google places on itself. Google has never explained itself or made any commitment to its users. Wouldn't you like to know what Google plans to do with everything it knows about you? Unfortunately, there's no way for you to find out. Google's plans for your private information are protected under commercial law. Google owns your data and is not required to explain what it may or may not do with all that knowledge.

Google is not alone in collecting every bit of data it can find on its users. Most companies these days are in the business of data collection. Think of every company doing business online: Amazon, Facebook, LinkedIn, and many smaller companies. Even brick-and-mortar companies like pharmacies or groceries use loyalty programs to track every purchase you make. In a 2012 *New York Times* article, Charles Duhigg tells the story of how Target knew about a sixteen-year-old girl's pregnancy, by piecing together her online-shopping history, even before her father knew. Banks and credit-card companies have massive amounts of data on you too, as do health insurers, doctors, and hospitals. Although banks and health providers are not allowed to hand over that data to another party, nothing stops them from using that data themselves in economic transactions with you. The race is on to know everything about you. And it's not something companies are making obvious, in case they stir public outrage and unleash a backlash. Before the public wakes up, companies are racing to develop data streams they alone control and own.

Companies employ many clever ways of collecting your data. Typically, companies say more data helps them offer you better products and services. But you rarely hear them explain how it benefits them. And rarely do they explain exactly how they're using your data. Online companies offer free services mostly to entice you to sign up, use the service, and in the process provide companies with tons of personal information. Once you're hooked or the service becomes an important part of your online life, they have a reliable data stream. Now some companies like Google are catching on to growing privacy concerns and trying to offer services that nominally promote privacy. But not necessarily from the companies offering the service.

Look at Google's encryption tool for Gmail, launched in mid-2014. For those worried about privacy, Google says this change helps ensure Gmail can't be read by anyone other than the intended recipient. Sounds like a win for privacy advocates, right? But there's a catch. In order for encryption to work, both the sender and the receiver must use it. That includes not just Gmail users but everyone they exchange e-mails with. So Google's new product could mean as much for Google as for its users. Getting more users onto Gmail would be another step in Google's long march to dominate e-mail. But Google will still read your e-mails. The encryption tool doesn't change that. It just makes it harder for competitors to do what Google is doing.

If companies are not collecting data themselves, they can readily buy it. Data brokers gather consumer information both online and offline and sell it to prospective employers, insurers, or companies that want to sell us things. In 2014 the Federal Trade Commission (FTC) studied nine data brokers, including Acxiom, CoreLogic, Datalogix, eBureau, ID Analytics, Intelius, PeekYou, Rapleaf, and Recorded Future. These companies gather our information from sources as varied as voter registrations, bankruptcy filings, in-store purchases, online purchases, online searches, and warranty registrations. The FTC found that "while each data broker source may provide only a few data elements about a consumer's activities, data brokers can put all of these data elements together to form a more detailed composite of the consumer's life." One of the nine brokers had 3,000 items of information for virtually every single consumer in the United States. The brokers then categorize consumers according to their race, ethnicity, economic status, health, marital status, family size, and many other types of personal groupings. These categories are then used to generate lists of people sharing similar characteristics, and those lists can be sold to companies. So whether companies collect data on their own or simply buy data from others, they have access to vast troves of information that are not accessible to consumers.

Learning to Manipulate Our Behavior

Behind the scenes, companies experiment with us, but rarely do we find out. And rarer still do we learn what they find after analyzing the results. When it comes to using personal data—if you can imagine it, somebody is already trying to do it. And they're not waiting around to get your approval or anyone else's approval, for that matter. Often, research teams within companies answer to no one, not even company executives, but operate according to their own agendas. It's not uncommon to find researchers who are tone deaf to privacy or other concerns of users. Christian Rudder, the cofounder of OkCupid, a popular dating website, put any doubt to rest on the topic when he wrote in his blog in July 2014: "Guess what, everybody: if you use the internet, you're the subject of hundreds of experiments at any given time, on every site. That's how websites work."

OkCupid ran several experiments to see whether providing users with different information would affect their behaviors. In one case the company hid profile pictures. In another case it hid profile text. In yet another it purposely lied, telling users who were good matches for a relationship that they were actually bad matches and telling users who were bad matches for a relationship that they were good matches. According to the results of the last test, users who thought they had found a good match were almost twice as likely to send more messages as those who thought they had found a bad match. These tests were conducted without users' knowledge. Companies cover their tracks by claiming they are testing new products and trying to enhance the services they provide.

But did Mr. Rudder feel any remorse for treating users like guinea pigs to learn about their behavior? Of course not. After all, the experiments were for the greater good: to make OkCupid work better, and—not incidentally—to make the company more valuable. The head of General Motors once said, "What's good for America is good for GM, and vice versa." Today that view is widespread. What's good for OkCupid is good for everyone, right? If a few individuals "match" poorly, that's a small price to pay.

Facebook has been caught experimenting on users too. The experiments actually were conducted two years before they were discovered, and Facebook only admitted it publicly after its researchers published their findings. The researchers chose 700,000 English-speaking Facebook users, without their knowledge, to conduct a series of experiments into whether their emotions could be manipulated. The researchers found that if you manipulate what users see in their news feed, their emotions will change to match. The company apologized and then tweaked its terms-of-service agreement, adding a research component to cover future research projects on its users. Facebook acknowledges that it has a group, called the Data Science Team, dedicated to experimenting on users.

Both OkCupid's and Facebook's relatively crude experiments reveal something important. They provide a glimpse of the fondest ambitions of the corporate sector: to manipulate behavior. Imagine how powerful a company could be if it could make you do something. Think of the impact if that were done on a large scale. Facebook's experiment also reveals that to manipulate emotion, you need the ability to detect emotion. Once Facebook can detect your emotions, it can understand and read you better than ever. The psychology of emotion is an intricate subject, but it's readily apparent that people are not always conscious of their emotions and often fail to see how their emotions affect their behaviors. Facebook is beginning to know users better than they know themselves.

The Growing Knowledge Gap

The knowledge gap results not just from companies knowing a lot more about us than we know about them, creating a profound asymmetry of information in the marketplace. It also means that the depth of what is known about consumers is unprecedented. The list of what is known about each one of us is daunting. Start with everything we do online. Whether you use Google Search or another search option, a simple Internet query instantly tells your location. It gives real-time clues to your state of mind, feelings, concerns, needs, and wants. What's more, your pattern of search indicates, with ever-improving exactness, your whole personality. That includes what you are thinking right now as well as a startlingly complete record of what you were thinking and doing at each moment in the past. Every word you read—newspapers, books, magazines, blogs, or e-mail—is noted. The "cloud"—that vast array of for-profit computers connected via the Internet—can tell what you know and what you are blind to. Everything you listen to or watch is recorded there. Who you communicate with and all that is said and left unsaid is stored and studied. What you like and dislike, your intimate desires, your shames, and your phobias can be detected, measured, and analyzed. And used. Your finances, taxes, medical status, emotional and psychological problems, relationships, addictions, and dishonesty are all laid bare in the cloud. All this data feeds predictive technology, the latest in predicting what you'll do when you are presented with a proposition.

Staying off the Internet isn't much better. Thanks to cell phones, your location is no secret. And Google has developed a phone that watches you all the time, ostensibly to serve you but meanwhile collecting reams of data. Where you've been, for how long, and even a pretty good idea of where you will go next is all there in the cloud. Everything you buy with a credit or debit card is there, and even should you pay cash, the remaining data may be rich enough to make excellent guesses about what you just bought. And it doesn't stop with cell phones. Even if you leave your phone at home, ubiquitous cameras and sensors with ever-improving biometric-recognition tools watch wherever you go. Stores examine how long you stand at each display and know whether you walk out without buying. Cues from your voice, keystrokes, clicks, facial expressions, and posture become valuable. The same goes for DNA. If a doctor takes your genetic sample, you may have a chance at keeping your genome out of commercial reach. Not so if a minute sample of saliva or the residue from a touch is captured in a store, a restaurant, or a bathroom. Not to mention the ever-improving ability to automatically separate and understand the words of single individuals in a crowded ballpark or restaurant via massive analytic programs or the almost magical abilities to see through clothes, listen through walls, smell infinitesimal scents, and decode DNA.

Virtually everything about us is known and collected by someone. Our impulse may be to try and escape from technology and the gaze of others. But the irony is that even while attempting to escape, we may be seen and known. When the database of what's known becomes sufficiently complete, what's left out can be deduced. Like a puzzle missing a piece, the contours of the "hole" in the data show what's missing. As data casts the light of knowledge, even the shadows where data doesn't reach can be exposed.

Meanwhile, the ability to store data is growing nearly as quickly as it is created. In practical terms, machines are observing every single thing that every single person does and recording it for as long as it is seen as useful. Outside of Bluffdale, Utah, half an hour from Salt Lake City, a secret complex roughly the size of a shopping mall began rising up in 2010. Virtually complete today, the National Security Agency's Utah Data Center includes space for the latest in supercomputers as well as thousands of technicians and analysts to operate them. No one is sure how much data it will hold, but estimates run into the exabytes—many thousands of times the size needed to record every book ever written in every language. And thanks to the magic of Moore's law, that capacity will likely double every couple of years.

Building the center wasn't cheap. Around $2 billion seems a good guess. But to build a machine that records and analyzes approximately everything that humans do, $2 billion isn't a lot of money. Compared to the $12 billion or so that Google makes in profits each year, it's quite affordable for our biggest companies.

So it should come as no surprise that Google and other Internet giants are building their own data repositories on a massive scale. There's a lot of data being created, and the rate of creating data is accelerating. All that data is stored where it can exist perpetually and be instantly recalled in perfect detail. Although each element of the data reservoir is trivial—a keystroke, a mouse click, a spoken word— taken as a whole, the data archive represents a granular record of thought and behavior unprecedented in human history.

Yet all that data becomes inconsequential if one can't derive meaning from it. That's where the magic of analytics comes in. Companies now can use everything they know about you to predict your behavior. At Google, for instance, the data tells its engineers what happened. As the data grows, they begin to understand why. And once they understand why, they can begin to guess what will happen next. Little by little, companies are gaining a power previously thought superhuman: to know the future.

The knowledge gap has been around since the beginning of industrialization. The growth of large selling organizations led to more knowledge being accumulated in the hands of sellers than buyers. But the Internet was supposed to change all that. Some thought the information revolution would give consumers greater knowledge and level the playing field with companies. But it's not turning out that way. Consumers are at a profound disadvantage. They lack the resources to match companies, and they don't have the scale or depth of information. As a result, companies know far more about us than we can ever hope to know about them or their products, and that gap grows every day.

You can see how industries like insurance, for instance, use predictive-behavior modeling from all of our personal data available to companies. In an August 2014 article on McKinsey's website, the management consultant explains how data analytics is changing the personal auto-insurance business:

> Instead of relying only on internal data sources such as loss histories, which was the norm, auto insurers started to incorporate behavior-based credit scores from credit bureaus into their analysis when they became aware of empirical evidence that people who pay their bills on time are also safer drivers. Although the use of credit scores in private-auto-insurance underwriting has been a contentious issue for the industry with consumer groups, the addition of behavioral and third-party sources was a significant leap forward from the claims histories, demographics, and physical data that insurers analyzed in the past.

What McKinsey is excited about is that insurance companies can make more money by knowing more about each customer. "With much better access to third-party data from a wide variety of sources, insurers can pose new questions and better understand many different types of risks. For example, which combination of geodemographic factors and treatment options will have the biggest impact on the life expectancies of people with Parkinson's disease? Which combination of corporate behaviors in health and safety management is predictive of lower worker-compensation claims? What is the probability that, within a given geographic radius, a person will die from a car accident or lose his or her house in a flood?" McKinsey is saying that with better data, insurers will be able to charge more precisely or price products at the maximum price a consumer would be willing to pay. The knowledge gap is playing out so that in any given economic transaction, those with knowledge can make more money and those with less knowledge are vulnerable.

The knowledge gap is made even greater by more and more information sources being held privately while public information gathering is cut back. These days, every company can buy software to gather information about its customers. And it can use services like Kaggle to get analytics experts to derive meaning from that information. As it becomes cheaper to gather data and analyze it for meaning, more companies are able to do so. But that information remains the property of the company and is kept private. Sometimes companies with access to marketable data streams will sell that data. Think of surveys of consumers or data on research on particular industries. As private sources of information explode, data sources available to the public are shrinking or becoming obsolete. In the United States in particular, data gathering for public use is not a priority. Think of our economic data, for instance. There's been a data revolution everywhere, but you won't see it in our economic statistics. Government spending cuts mean that government agencies spend less and less money just trying to do the same thing. The private sector now holds the real-time sources of information on the economy. Think of what credit-card companies know about consumer spending. Their information, with its laserlike focus and real-time accuracy, is far more useful than any government data on consumer spending.

The trend of more information in private hands is playing out in other ways too. A recent story on the *New York Times* website about big data research offered a small window into the dramatic change taking place. One of the researchers, Gary King, director of Harvard University's Institute for Quantitative Social Science, noted: "It used to be that academics has way more data than companies. But that has flipped now." Academics usually release their findings and data to the public in the form of working papers or journal papers. Companies typically do not, which means that more and more data is being walled off from the public.

The data revolution gives us the illusion of lots of knowledge. And unquestionably, consumers have far more information now at our fingertips than ever before. But think about what kind of information we have. We can click on any website and find out anything about cooking, travel, clothes, entertainment—you name it—but try finding information about economic matters. How do you know if you're getting paid fairly, for instance, or if those wine glasses you just purchased were sold to you at a fair price? Only your boss knows the answer for sure—or a seller of wine glasses. Where do you even go to try and find that out?

The endless information on the Internet doesn't help us with money matters. That's because much of that information is walled off from us. Think of cell phones. How do you get good comparisons on your cell-phone plan? Or pharmaceuticals? Who is even collecting and disseminating information to help consumers these days? It's certainly not something the government does much of. And it's certainly not something the private sector does, with the exception of some travel sites. But even then, the sites offer comparisons for you. They don't show you what everyone else is paying for the same trip. And ironically, when you search for more information, that search is then known, recorded, and used by others like Google to know you even better.

The digital age has tipped the balance of knowledge in the corporate world's favor. A major shift in the marketplace is underway. Power in economic transactions is accumulating in the hands of companies, and that power is playing out commercially against consumers. The cost of individual haggling over transactions has dropped to nearly zero as sellers can easily find out all about individual consumers and offer prices or discounts tailored to what they think the consumer will pay. So instead of guessing, sellers can charge precisely the highest price each customer would willingly pay, capturing the consumer surplus entirely. Such a significant knowledge advantage means the benefits that used to be shared between consumers and sellers will be going to the seller.

Sellers are fast approaching godlike omniscience—never before have they had the ability to know everything about you. And the prospect that they soon will know more about you than even you do is growing. As companies know how much you're willing to pay, as well as the extent of your financial resources, they will possess the unique ability to make you pay. In some circumstances, *all you can pay*.

PART II

What Companies Do with Data

4

A Special Price Just for You

From as early as John Monro could remember, he aspired to go to college. His father, a graduate of Harvard University, was a chemist, and his mother was the daughter of a mill owner. But the family was not prosperous, and Monro needed financial assistance to attend the schools he dreamed about. It was the late 1920s, and Monro, a teenager growing up in North Andover, Massachusetts, worked hard to distinguish himself academically. He first won a scholarship to Phillips Academy in Andover, and then another in the 1930s to attend Harvard. Back then, colleges and universities gave scholarships based on need and whether the candidate seemed deserving or exceptional. In large part, scholarships were community driven. If you were a clergyman's son, for instance, or the child of a faculty member, or your father was an upstanding member of the community, you stood a good chance of winning a scholarship to study at your local college or university. But no systematic approach to financial aid existed. Each university had its own way of awarding tuition scholarships.

Today, colleges and universities around the country all use the same method to calculate what's called *financial aid*. It's the same method devised by John Monro some sixty-five years ago.

Monro didn't set out to get into the business of financial aid. While at Harvard he read widely about Karl Marx and communism and was inspired by the ideas of social justice and equality that were prevalent at the time. He was attracted to journalism and worked to develop a newspaper to rival the *Harvard Crimson*, which he believed was too conservative. After graduating in 1935, he worked for Harvard, writing press releases, and for the *Boston Transcript* as a reporter. During World War II, he served in the navy in the Pacific and was awarded the Bronze Star Medal for distinguished service. When Monro returned from the war, a Harvard administrator convinced him to join the university as an adviser to veterans taking advantage of the GI Bill of Rights to attend college. From that position, Monro took over as director of financial aid for the university in the early 1950s.

It was in this role that Monro devised the first-ever rule for granting financial aid. To determine what a student should pay for college, Monro and a committee would calculate 15 percent of the family's after-tax income and then subtract an amount for each additional child at school: $100 for a child at public school; $200 for one at private school. Monro's approach relied on some key assumptions: first, that it was the parents' responsibility to send their child to college; and second, that the cost of college should be based on parents' ability to pay. Monro himself believed his method was efficient, useful, and reasonably fair, but he also recognized its limitations: It did not take into account a family's assets or savings or even the applicant's own earnings.

Over the next few years, Monro kept refining his system, requiring more and more financial information from parents. In 1953 the College Board convened some of the best minds on the topic to present papers on the policies and the procedures for awarding scholarships. This was Monro's chance to unveil his method for granting financial aid to the rest of the country. He presented what he described at the time as "a reliable, careful system for measuring and comparing" the needs of applicants. Monro's paper stood out.

According to Monro, there were two key factors to understand before granting financial aid: the true cost of attending college and the applicant's resources. He calculated that the cost of attending Harvard was not just tuition (some $800 at the time) but fees, room and board, books, personal expenses, and limited travel. So the true cost could be as high as $1,200 to $1,400.

Next, he calculated an applicant's resources. And on that score, Monro did something no other college or university did at the time. He determined an applicant's resources by using a complicated calculation requiring detailed knowledge of a family's financial situation. In his paper he outlined the need for thorough information regarding parents' employment, all sources of income, assets, savings and debt, itemized business expenses, federal income taxes, extraordinary expenses, and all dependents. After collecting that information, he determined a "calculated contribution." Monro believed that above all else, establishing the calculated contribution was critical to determining financial need.

As a result of the conference, the College Board introduced a number of new initiatives. It announced a central information service for applicants known as the College Scholarship Service. This gave applicants a single form to fill out revealing parents' detailed financial information that could be shared with colleges and universities. And by 1957 a national system for determining financial aid had been put in place, based on Monro's formula for calculating a family's expected contribution. In 1958 the National Defense Education Act was passed into law, and that formalized the process.

Today the basic mechanics of the system devised all those years ago remain in place. Students and their parents fill out a standard financial aid form that is shared with colleges and universities. These forms require parents to answer detailed questions about their financial resources: how much money they earn in taxed and untaxed income, the value of their assets, any government benefits they receive, the size of the family, and the number of children in college. The school then calculates an applicant's expected family contribution. Once it has a dollar figure, it deducts that number from the full tuition price of the institution to determine the amount of financial aid to award the applicant.

The system was unquestionably well intended. But during the stress of the college admission process, families don't often stop to think about what's actually happening. While the applicant writes essays describing his or her remarkable achievements, parents provide financial aid offices with every significant detail about the family finances. It's remarkable how much private financial information families willingly hand over to colleges. Of course, there's no choice. That's the only way a student can be awarded financial aid.

So when it comes to college and university tuition, there's an advertised price and then there's the real price—the one you actually pay. That price is calculated just for you, according to your own unique financial situation. At the beginning of the college process, most families have no idea what the cost will end up being. Rough numbers are available, of course. Colleges and universities all list an advertised price for tuition and room and board on their websites. Then there are rough averages. On average, tuition costs $25,000 at public colleges and $35,000 at private colleges. But if your child is interested in a particular school and you want to know whether you can afford it, good luck figuring out the price.

Take Princeton University, for example. You can easily find its advertised price of $58,965. That includes tuition, room and board, and miscellaneous costs for the 2014–2015 academic year. And although Princeton and some others now offer an online calculator to estimate your amount of financial aid, there's no way to tell the price you will end up paying without investing time and effort into a detailed application.

The way colleges and universities calculate the price you pay depends on obliging you to disclose the details of your family situation and financial resources. Armed with that knowledge and considering its own budget, the school sets the final price to collect as much of the advertised price as the student and the family can together afford. What colleges call financial aid is nothing more than a discount. A federal financial-aid application reveals to the school your entire financial picture in order to calculate the expected family contribution. Your expected family contribution boils down to the maximum price the admissions office guesses each applicant will agree to pay. So if you ask a college how much it costs to attend, you won't get a straight answer. Before they respond, colleges ask how much money you can afford to spend. What's even more remarkable is that parents find out the final price only after their child accepts an offer to attend. By that time, the family is well down the road to a decision about whether or not to attend. At that point it's hard to say no.

Other industries work like colleges in that way. Think of health care. Patients typically don't know the price until the care has been completed and they're discharged. After your knee has been replaced, it's a bit late to say you want something cheaper. Or think of banking. Only after you hand over your financial information, earnings, assets, and credit history will banks confirm what your mortgage will actually cost. At that point, borrowers may not be eager to start over with another bank.

Colleges are clever marketers: They sell exclusive, branded products that many believe are all but essential. And then they use customer information to calculate the maximum price they can charge. In economics that's called *price discrimination*, which happens when customers receive identical products but pay different prices for them, as determined by the seller. Instead of charging one price to all, colleges and universities essentially customize the price for every individual.

The philosophy of charging as much as the college applicant can afford doesn't apply only to the low to middle end of the income spectrum. Those who can easily afford the tuition feel a not-so-subtle pressure to "donate" above and beyond that base fee to the school. It's no mere coincidence that big givers tend to see their children enrolled at Princeton. After all, Princeton didn't accumulate its huge endowment by accident. So at higher income levels, the price of college can actually exceed the advertised price.

The point is not that colleges and universities are doing something wrong. They're just acting in their own interest. After all, the price discrimination system started out as a well-intentioned way to help needy students. Most colleges and universities try to make college as valuable as possible while still remaining accessible to families of limited means. That's clear on campuses like Princeton's, where a large proportion of students receive some kind of financial aid. But there's no doubt that college prices have risen faster than most other items and that colleges very effectively extract money from middle-class families.

What's fascinating is that colleges and universities use the technique of price discrimination to determine their pricing. It's a very powerful means of separating people from their money. And in the case of colleges and universities, it's not just about separating families from their current assets. Through student debt, colleges absorb future earnings as well. With total outstanding student loans now over $1 trillion in the United States, colleges and universities take into account how much students can earn in the future when calculating the price of college and university today.

What if colleges and universities didn't continually raise prices while providing individual discounts and instead adopted uniform pricing for all? In that case they would have to set the price at the lowest common denominator in order to fill all their seats. The college's list price would actually mean something because it would represent the fair market value of the service. And overall, colleges would have to make do with lower tuition receipts.

Think about what an advantage colleges and universities hold when they know precisely how much each customer can afford to pay. What if their sole aim was to make as much profit as they could from every student? Luckily for most parents, the goal of colleges and universities is not to profit as much as they can. Most schools roughly break even or suffer modest losses that get covered by alumni support. But think about what other businesses could do using this technique that colleges have validated. There's little doubt sellers would charge customers the most they could afford to pay.

Price discrimination, after all, is a very useful tool for collecting surplus. It's been around for a long time and is commonly used by companies throughout the world. But until recently it was impossible for most sellers to accurately assess just how much individual buyers can afford to pay for a particular product.

The Discount Game

Nobody is about to hand over their financial details to Walmart (knowingly, anyway). Retailers and service providers—in fact anyone selling anything—would love to have a detailed picture of the buyer's resources. Think of airlines, for example. Once upon a time, you could just look up the price of a ticket from New York to Los Angeles. That changed a long time ago. Now prices shift from moment to moment, and airlines use various techniques to gauge just how badly you want to fly and how much you care about price. The "Saturday night stay" requirement for lower fares was a crude but fairly effective way of discriminating between business and leisure travelers. The result was that passengers on exactly the same flights paid different prices based solely on where they spent the weekend. Or look at direct flights. Even though the actual cost of a direct flight is generally lower than that of two connecting flights, passengers who prefer direct flights may find there's a premium to pay for the convenience. It's typical now for equivalent seats to the same destination to cost vastly different amounts depending on a multitude of factors like these.

Price discrimination appears throughout our economy in consumer products, markets, telecommunications, travel, transport, finance, and banking. Pharmaceutical and medical-device companies, for instance, have long sold the same drugs or products globally at different prices, usually charging higher prices in the United States and lower prices in Europe and elsewhere. A report released in 2014 by the International Federation of Health Plans revealed that common medicines consistently cost more in the United States than in Europe. Grocery stores and drugstores also typically discriminate on price. It's not uncommon for retailers to print different prices in their catalogs for higher-income neighborhoods versus lower-income neighborhoods. In fact, virtually every industry now engages in some form of price discrimination. We often don't even think about price discrimination because it occurs everywhere, in multiple forms and degrees.

Unlike most of the public, companies think about price discrimination all the time. The most powerful kind of price discrimination is what colleges practice. Using individual data, they charge the maximum price each consumer is willing to pay. Previously, colleges and universities held a unique position, with privileged access to financial and wealth information that other businesses could only wish for. Most companies, with the exception of banks, had to settle for educated guesswork rather than certainty. Although colleges lead the way in the most powerful type of price discrimination, other industries like airlines are now catching up because of ever-improving data collection and analysis technologies. Although airlines don't review our tax returns and bank statements, they constantly search for other clues to tell them how to price their products, setting different prices for each customer.

Charging different prices depending on the quantity consumed represents another common form of price discrimination practiced in retail. At a local liquor store, a bottle of ordinary table wine normally costs seven dollars. If you buy two bottles, they cost a total of twelve dollars, or six dollars each. And three bottles cost fifteen dollars, dropping the price to five dollars each. It's not a matter of the seller's cost. The bottles all cost the seller the same amount. But different quantities appeal to different segments of the market, and the price varies accordingly. Price discrimination based on the quantity consumed occurs everywhere in the economy, but it's particularly apparent in bulk-discount stores, grocery stores, and pharmacies.

Offering slight variations in the product is another way to discriminate on price. Think back to General Motors and cars. When a customer buys a car, slight variations in the car can lead to big variations in price. You want a sunroof? Nice, but it will cost you. Leather seats or an upgrade to the fancy entertainment and audio system? All the little extras add up to big variations in the price of the car.

Sometimes price discrimination is overtly based on age. Senior, child, and student discounts are common in movie theaters and other leisure and entertainment locations where it generally doesn't cost the seller much to accommodate an additional customer.

Temporary sales and discounts are ingrained into our retail culture. Think of the "Black Friday" sales on the Friday after Thanksgiving. Stores know the frenzy attracts price-sensitive shoppers who will come and brave the crowds while others will shop at a calmer time and buy at full price. Much of the time, retailers keep prices high to capture revenue from shoppers willing to pay up, and then for very brief periods offer sales to capture shoppers who react to discounts.

Coupons represent another tool for price discrimination. In this case, a customer with a coupon gets charged a lower price than one who walks in off the street. The secret is that it takes time and effort to work the coupon system. Busy, affluent people value their time too much to clip coupons and wind up paying a higher price. Even better for retailers, some people, although secretly tempted to use coupons, are reluctant to because they want to be perceived as busy and affluent even if the discount matters to them.

Customer loyalty programs, which have grown enormously in recent years, provide yet another way to adjust pricing. In addition to collecting consumer data, loyalty programs deliver targeted discounts when the retailer sees a reason to. Frequent-flier, hotel, and car-rental loyalty programs led the way, and now grocery stores and pharmacies have gotten into the game. Even coffee shops and bookstores offer their own loyalty programs now.

Companies shrewdly frame the issue as one of discounting. Sales, special prices, discounts, and rewards all make it seem as if customers are getting a great deal. Who doesn't love a discount? But in fact, if one customer pays less than another for the same thing, somebody's deal turns out not to be so good. The ability to discount is also the ability to charge customers more whenever the situation allows. In a world teeming with discounts, it's become very hard to determine the real market price. Companies never explicitly say they're charging others a different price but they obviously do. Sellers imply that customers are getting a special price, sometimes even a price "just for you." Consumers are so used to finding discounts and deals, they've stopped thinking about what it all means.

When you go into CVS Pharmacy and use your CVS member card to shop, not every product is offered at a discount. Some items you need might be, but others are priced higher than you would like. A system that manages discounting is a system that manages surcharges. And after all, if sellers know you want the product, why should they cut you a break, especially when you can't wait until it goes on sale? When you run out of toothpaste and head to CVS, you may or may not find your brand of toothpaste on sale. But when there's absolutely nothing left in the tube, you'll pay up if you have to.

Consumers accept price discrimination as an ordinary part of the landscape because they can't resist the appeal. The idea that we might get a low price is tempting, maybe even more so if we feel others get a worse deal. But how much do consumers really know? It wouldn't be easy to compare your expenditures with your best friend's, even if you were willing to take the trouble. So many variables exist—brands, products, sizes, varieties—that consumers can only guess at where the "market" price lies. Sellers, on the other hand, hold all the cards. Unlike consumers, they actually know what people are paying, and they manage pricing accordingly.

Look more closely at loyalty programs, for instance. In the United States, they're often called discount cards, club cards, or rewards cards. They are pitched to make consumers feel special, promising desirable rewards. But loyalty-program data can signal to the seller that you already like a particular product, and you're not shopping around. In that case, a seller feels no pressure to offer you the best deal. Think about how it works. When you sign up, you provide the retailer with loads of personal information, establishing a profile. From then on the retailer keeps track of what you buy, and when, and for how much. That insight into your behavior is valuable. When companies figure out just how loyal you really are, they can charge what they want because they know you don't want to go elsewhere.

Think of what happens in a car-rental loyalty program. The rental agency knows a few key things about someone who signs up for its loyalty-rewards program. First, the customer probably rents cars a lot. In general, that fits the mold of business people, who care more about convenience than price. When they rent a car, they're in a hurry and don't want to stand at the counter waiting for hours to do the paperwork. And because the customer's employer foots the bill, he or she doesn't really care about getting the best price. Second, the customer already knows and trusts the rental agency. Putting the pieces together, the customer probably is not likely to shop around. So when the customer visits the agency website to book a car for a one-day midweek rental to pick up at the airport, it should come as no surprise that the resulting price quote is actually higher than if that same loyal customer had searched through an anonymous price-comparison website.

Retailers have put a lot of energy into devising loyalty programs in recent years. It's hard to enter a supermarket or pharmacy that doesn't have some kind of program. And if you notice, such programs make it much harder to read and understand the price of products. Take CVS, for instance. Stop in to buy headache medicine, and you'll find it's not a quick decision if you care about price. One brand offers buy two, get 50 percent off the second; another offers a dollar discount; a third offers a buy one, get one free; and a fourth offers a buy one, get 50 percent off your next purchase. Yet another item is the generic store brand, which may be just as good—or may not. All those varied prices are obscured by different strengths, different ingredients, and different quantities in each bottle. How can a consumer hope to figure out which is the best value? Then add into the mix the customer loyalty programs that may give a little cash back or provide some coupons on unrelated products, and finally, multiply this by the number of different retailers within striking range. It's enough to make your headache even worse!

Early research on loyalty programs in the 1990s by Frederick Reichheld and W. Earl Sasser found that loyal customers buy more and pay higher prices. And they came up with a rule of thumb that shows a 5 percent increase in customer retention increases a company's profitability by 25 percent. No wonder we've seen a proliferation of loyalty programs! The more a customer shops with one seller, the more the business knows about the customer, making it easier to personalize products, services, and prices for that customer.

With the rise of advanced data analytics, grocery loyalty programs are getting more sophisticated. Supermarket chains like Safeway and Kroger use data based on a customer's shopping history to offer personalized deals and coupons. "There's going to come a point where our shelf pricing is pretty irrelevant because we can be so personalized in what we offer people," Safeway CEO Steve Burd told the Associated Press in 2013. In the same article, Euan White, an executive with a firm that helps supermarkets use consumer data to increase profitability, said: "The price offered to the individual customer is really between the retailer and customer now. Loyalty programs just for you are an easy way to move to personalized pricing where each one of us, on our own, must negotiate with the seller."

Fast Pricing

Combine the long-standing practices of price discrimination with advanced technology and you arrive at *dynamic pricing*. Using the system first pioneered by airlines, sellers of virtually anything can instantly change the price they offer to an individual customer. In business parlance, we are increasingly seeing a 121 (meaning "one-to-one") proposition based on the seller's calculations of the customer's willingness to pay. A seller applies all the information it has collected about the individual, everything from basic demographics to past purchase history. Staples, for example, uses zip codes to offer different prices. Customers in wealthy neighborhoods presumably are charged more, and in neighborhoods where there is a competitor, pricing can be more competitive. In the online world, the price of products fluctuates from moment to moment, for everything ranging from airline tickets to toilet paper.

In an episode reported a few years back, an Amazon customer found that after removing the cookies on his computer, he got substantially lower prices on his DVD purchases. Amazon denied engaging in individualized pricing, explaining it away as a random price test. Customer tracking is a common practice in many industries. In the airline industry, for example, read the blogs about how to outfox airlines to get the lowest price and you'll find that some advocate clearing your browser before you shop for a ticket so the airline can't tell who it's dealing with. Companies tend to be very quiet, even a bit defensive, about how they price their products. That's because they know the public doesn't like the idea of individualized price discrimination. Who wants to feel like they can be ripped off at any time? Everybody loves a discount, but nobody wants to pay twice as much as someone else. So companies keep their cards close to the vest and say as little as possible.

Yet over time, consumers have become acclimatized to some forms of price discrimination. Airline pricing has resembled casino gambling for so long that customers seem to grudgingly accept it. Most people who fly these days accept that the person next to them probably paid a different price. Like gambling, perhaps they like a system that sometimes offers a "win." But the gambling analogy is apt in another sense: Customers occasionally do well, but over time, the house always wins.

Some organizations already know very intimate personal information about their customers. Colleges, banks, and hospitals can gauge what they offer and what they charge based on very detailed knowledge about customers. Many ethical organizations limit how they use this information. But in general, there's little to stop them from pushing prices higher in individual cases. And even when organizations refrain from using information they could otherwise profit from, it's worth thinking about just how strong and how secure those ethical barriers are.

The problem for consumers is that barriers to our information are falling fast. Although we used to share financial information only with banks and other trusted advisers, now a lot of financial information we never expected to reveal is available for a fee from data brokers.

In addition, financial information is collected online. The technology used by Google and Facebook is in its infancy in many ways, but it's plausible that they and other large Internet data players will be able to piece together a very clear financial picture of each one of us. Change is arriving sooner than you may think. And once companies know everything they need to know about you, they can begin to calculate your willingness and ability to pay for every single thing in real time. Dynamic pricing has often been portrayed in favorable terms, along the lines of always giving customers the "best" price. The question consumers should ask is, best for whom? Sales, special prices, and discounts may make it seem as if customers get a special deal at a particular moment. But remember, a firm's ability to give an instant special deal is also the ability to charge you the maximum you are prepared to pay. The system clearly works both ways. And as the price of gathering, analyzing, and storing information drops, the cost of dynamic pricing falls as well, making it more and more economical.

The Economics of Price

Economists have long understood that price discrimination occurs when firms hold some degree of monopoly or market power, even if limited. In truly competitive markets, price discrimination can't occur because customers seek and get the lowest price. Raising prices for some customers doesn't work because customers able to get a low price can buy in quantity and then resell the product to others. In that case, firms are price takers rather than price setters because they must settle for what the market will bear. But in markets in which firms can set the price, they can also discriminate on price. And it's very rare to find perfectly competitive markets. The information gap alone is sufficiently large enough that most companies enjoy at least some degree of market power and some ability to discriminate on price. Think back to Princeton. Although the United States contains many universities, there's only one Princeton. So in a sense, Princeton is its own little monopoly. If you really want a Princeton education, you take the price Princeton gives you. Every significant brand shares a similar characteristic. You can find cheaper cola, but if you want Coke, you have to pay what Coke charges.

In addition to a degree of market power, other factors need to be in place for one-to-one price negotiation. Whenever firms discriminate between customers, a secondary market would quickly even out prices. The customer who can get the lowest price would turn around and resell to everybody else. So where resale is possible, firms often try to restrict or prohibit the transferability of their products. Think of how airlines do it. There's no good reason for airfares to be non-transferable but they are. You may hear airlines justify why tickets cannot be transferred on the basis of security, but they have many ways of handling name changes that won't compromise our security. The true reason is so you can't buy a low-priced fare and sell it to your neighbor. If we could resell airline tickets, fares would quickly level out significantly. Firms must also be able to identify different segments of the market and learn how much different segments want or need the product. To keep customers from knowing when they are being charged more, the different segments need to be kept separate, either physically or in time or by category of use, such as a teacher's edition of a textbook versus a student's edition. Another example would be to introduce a new book or iPhone at full price and then later bring out lower-priced editions. Those wanting to be first pay the higher price.

All price discrimination has a single aim: capturing surplus from consumers. "Firms know that some people can and will pay more," said Steve Pressman, an economist at Monmouth University. "To engage in price discrimination and extract some of the consumer surplus they first need to find the people who would pay more and then charge higher prices to those people." Professor Pressman typically explains it this way to his class: "A simple example of price discrimination is the cost of haircuts. Men, who often don't care very much how they look (and sometimes don't even have much hair!) are generally willing to pay less for haircuts than women, who generally care a great deal about their hair. Charging women more than men extracts some of the consumer surplus. Depending on your point of view it isn't fair, but it is relatively easy to do in practice." To make up for the difference, women's haircuts tend to include more "service"— for example, a relaxing massage and hair wash and a more attentive blow-dry at the end. In practice, though, the difference in service can be small while the price varies greatly.

Price discrimination offers a huge opportunity for sellers, and only in rarer cases can buyers benefit. It all depends on the seller's intention. In the case of Princeton, low-income families who could otherwise not afford to pay Princeton's full tuition price get a break. Assuming that Princeton's list price is fair (plausible though far from certain), the university takes a bath on financial aid. But a traveller who for personal reasons suddenly has to buy a ticket to fly from New York to Paris and ends up paying twice the regular price loses out. Price discrimination is all about making customers pay the most they're willing to pay, allowing firms to capture every last dollar of revenue available. On the whole, that's great for companies but comes at the expense of customers. The proliferation of price discrimination creates a different reality in the marketplace: Instead of a mass market in which millions of consumers are in the same boat, it's just you, on your own, against the world.

Two main effects are associated with widespread price discrimination. First, it tends to lead to higher overall prices. College and university tuition is a good example. Since 1969 the average cost of college has almost doubled compared to median family income, according to the National Center for Education Statistics and the Census Bureau. That cost includes tuition, fees, and room and board for full-time students at degree-granting institutions, including both public and private colleges and universities. In 1969 the average cost came to $9,502 after adjusting for inflation, according to the National Center for Education Statistics. By 2012 the cost averaged $19,339. Because a typical family earns $51,017, the U.S. median income, college tuition for just one child will absorb almost 40 percent of its income. That's a big increase from the 20 percent of typical family income in 1969. Of course, the price of college varies greatly depending on where you go and whether the institution is public or private. Almost three-quarters of Americans attend public universities and colleges, where costs have risen quickly but still remain far lower than at private institutions. In 1969 public colleges and universities charged an average of $7,206 compared to $14,292 in 2012, after adjusting for inflation. In comparison, private institutions averaged $15,329 back in 1969 versus $33,047 in 2012.

What's behind the rise? Several factors. For starters, administration costs have grown strongly on most campuses. In part, this has to do with an explosion in applications and enrollments, requiring more resources. But salaries of administrators, particularly those in charge, seem out of line with the rest of the institution. It's not unheard of for the president of a large university's compensation to approach $1 million. Meanwhile, campuses have seen a boom in infrastructure spending to upgrade student facilities like gyms, student centers, and dorms. The building boom seems almost like an arms race in which institutions compete against each other on state-of-the-art fitness centers. Cutbacks in public spending on education have also led to tuition hikes at public colleges and universities as they try to keep pace with private schools in terms of both paying their administration and upgrading campus facilities.

Ask any economist, though, and you will find that price discrimination plays a critical role in rising tuition. The financial-aid system that allows colleges and universities to discriminate on price makes it easy to raise the list price. Schools don't have to worry that some of their customers won't be able to attend or that they won't sell all their seats. They can charge whatever list price they want because many, and sometimes most, won't actually pay that price. Harvard brags that 70 percent of its students receive some form of financial aid. That means two out of three students don't pay the advertised price. When sellers no longer compete on price, they feel no pressure to keep prices down. And higher prices bring higher tuition revenues. The effect shows up only at the upper end of the range because students of lesser means pay the same as they always do: all they can afford. More affluent students, though, pay the ever-increasing list price. Taken to the logical extreme, schools could do away with list prices entirely and take the same percentage of family wealth from each newly admitted student.

There's another problem with the pricing system. Because of its combination of brand recognition and its widespread perception of prestige, Harvard's tuition price (the list price, not the prices students actually pay) is an important benchmark for the list price at other schools. If another school wants to charge more than Harvard, it's going to have to explain itself. But if a school charges less, that's a tacit admission that it just doesn't measure up. So the list prices of private colleges tend to follow the leader.

Price discrimination casts a fog around the market price. High school seniors receive limited information about what students actually pay at the schools they are considering. At first, all they can see is the list price. Then, after going through a fairly involved application process, they finally see the actual price. When you search Expedia for an airline ticket from Los Angeles to Melbourne, you see only the price offered to you. Expedia doesn't reveal what everyone else pays. How are consumers supposed to figure out whether they are paying the "market" price or an arbitrary price made up just for them? Even if consumers consult information on average prices, they're not much better off. The very concept of statistical analysis depends on variation, and the consumer can't keep up. To create a level negotiating field, the consumer must somehow access real-time data about flight searches and ticket purchases, collect a substantial body of data on airline behavior, and then feed it all into a powerful analytic engine that can predict the best course of action. None of that is about to happen, so consumers make do with price-comparison websites. That's better than nothing, but it's not a level playing field. Airlines have precise information about what everyone pays and leaves consumers mostly in the dark. In a classic divide-and-conquer strategy, price discrimination separates consumers from each other and keeps them in the dark about the market. Airlines are just the tip of the iceberg. In virtually every type of market, pricing is getting trickier, more complicated, and less transparent. All these gimmicks and strategies create the equivalent of dark pools where only those in the know have access to the full range of price data. When customers can't see what others are paying, sellers gain the upper hand. Consumers are forced to take the offered price on faith. Price discrimination is an effective tool for emptying their pockets.

Companies are unapologetic about it because they see price discrimination as a normal part of doing business. There's nothing wrong with charging customers what something is worth to them, you may hear a corporate executive say. It's a free market, right? If they don't like it, they can buy from somebody else. And indeed, if the real world corresponded with the classical definition of a perfect market, there would be no problem. The trouble is, that's rarely the case. In an earlier age, when mass markets prevailed and consumers stuck up for their interests, price discrimination was termed "profiteering" or "price gouging." And the public still resists "price gouging," particularly in the wake of emergencies. In the aftermath of Hurricane Sandy in 2012, drivers lodged hundreds of complaints against gas stations and grocery stores for charging jacked-up prices. It's a good bet gas-station owners didn't feel as if they were doing anything wrong. In their view, they charged their customers precisely what it was worth to them to fill up their tanks. If they hadn't liked the price, they wouldn't have bought the gas. And after all, isn't everyone throughout the economy doing the same—charging as much as they can?

The idea of taking advantage of a disaster to make money is still too much for most Americans. Several states have enacted laws against price gouging during emergencies. It's recognized that consumers can be terribly vulnerable when they need basic supplies like gas. The tricky thing is determining what's reasonable or fair in practice. With the current way we price gas, drivers have some idea of where prices are at, so a sudden doubling or tripling of prices seems outrageous. But as loyalty systems and individual price discounts proliferate, stated prices will creep up while more and more customers will pay something less than the full advertised price. Eventually, drivers will no longer know the market price for gas. Online "gas finder" services might try to fill the gap, helping drivers avoid the most egregious situations. But objectivity will be a concern, and gas stations may elect not to participate.

Uber, the car-service company, is an interesting case. The company uses its computing power to set prices in real time, raising them when demand for rides is high and lowering them at other times. Customers use Uber as an online taxi service. When they need a ride, they use an app on their smartphones to calculate the price of the trip based on the demand at that point in time in their particular area or neighborhood. After Hurricane Sandy severely disrupted transport in New York City, the prices Uber charged spiked sharply, causing customers to complain. After two years of discussions with the New York attorney general, the car-ride company agreed to comply with basic price-gouging laws and said it would follow suit nationally as well.

Price-gouging laws, though, provide very little in the way of actual protection for consumers. They generally only apply during an official state of emergency: for example, a storm or earthquake that disrupts an entire community, or if an unfair price increase can't be explained by other factors. So the basic problem becomes one of judging what's fair, which is not easy. And even then, unless it's a widespread emergency, consumers are out of luck. If an emergency applies just to you—an illness, a fire, a family crisis—sellers remain free to charge as much as they can get.

States such as Florida, New York, and California have enacted "price-gouging" laws in times of emergencies, but in practice, violations can be difficult to prosecute. The federal government has a law on the books known as the Robinson-Patman Act that, on its face, seems to prevent price discrimination more broadly. However, the law contains a very important limitation. Price discrimination doesn't violate the act unless it tends to lessen competition or create a monopoly. That bit of legal gobbledygook means that it only applies to companies. So although the federal act might prevent discrimination against a company, consumers are out of luck. Companies can charge differing prices to individuals with impunity. A legal case back in 1996 is still talked about today. Consumers sued Victoria's Secret on the grounds that it distributed catalogs to its customers with different prices for the same products. Judge Robert W. Sweet of the U.S. District Court for the Southern District of New York dismissed the claims and, in a rare move, even imposed sanctions against the attorney for filing the suit in the first place.

Free-market advocates have long argued against price-gouging laws on the grounds that they interfere with the distribution of products and services. That philosophy has many adherents, but it doesn't reflect the real world. It rests on a transparent tautology. So long as one assumes a given market already fits the perfect mold, lo and behold there can never be a reason to try to improve it. Such thinking is easily debunked. There isn't, and there never has been, a perfect market. Imbalances in information, the ownership of key resources, the very real challenges of communication and transport, and the time-based nature of human needs prevent goods and services from flowing freely from sellers to purchasers at uniform, market-clearing prices. The real world presents many opportunities for sellers to make an extra buck. In the past most pricing opportunities were difficult to exploit because they tended to be particular to each individual and changed from moment to moment. But as sellers collect and take advantage of more and more information, they will miss fewer and fewer opportunities to profit. Individual buyers simply lack the resources and incentives to stay abreast of sellers.

Many people profess great faith in the ability of markets to allocate things fairly. After all, the thinking goes, if people are prepared to pay a high price, then that's what it's worth. Nobody's holding a gun to their heads, right? But of course that's exactly the problem. Consumers feel lots of pressure all the time: everything from the basic desire to stay alive to more complex desires for self-expression and esteem. Sometimes there *is* the full equivalent of a gun to the head. Most people wouldn't accept a scenario in which doctors and hospitals can charge whatever they want for lifesaving care. More often, a more subtle degree of pressure is involved. Imagine you are late for a meeting and a few minutes really matter to you. In that situation you pretty much have to accept what you are offered because you don't have time to shop for alternatives.

Without any constraints on price discrimination, consumer markets will gradually evolve into one-to-one markets in which sellers exploit opportunities to charge as much as possible. In the extreme, consumers will part with everything they have. The *Titanic* famously lacked sufficient lifeboat capacity for all its passengers. Just think how much the White Star Line could have raked in if it had charged what the market would bear for each seat in a lifeboat. If our economic system permits sellers to benefit from customer distress, we create a truly perverse incentive to allow, or even to cause, more and more situations that put consumers under pressure. It's not attractive to think of the *Titanic* as a profit center. It would be similarly offensive to create long lines at airport security to improve the sales of convenience items in airports.

Although economic theorists have considered the threat discriminatory pricing poses to the consumer surplus, most economists tend to overlook the issue. Mainstream neoclassical economic theory argues that price discrimination is merely a characteristic of an efficient market rather than a troubling concern. The thinking is that if companies can offer products at the price each customer wants to pay, then we will achieve an efficient allocation of resources in the economy. But that presupposes a level playing field. Consumers aren't in a good position to collect data on companies to exploit opportunities for savings. But companies are in an excellent position to charge consumers more. It's not a fair fight.

Economists hate to take fairness into account because it makes such a mess of their neat theories. On top of that, economists remain completely unprepared to deal with the new reality of price discrimination on a 121 basis in the age of big data and the end of privacy. Most studies of the effects of price discrimination on consumer prices dismiss the type of price discrimination practiced by colleges and universities as something that could never happen elsewhere in the economy. "This would require you to read consumers' minds and see inside their wallets," wrote Scott A. Wolla, a senior economic education specialist, in a newsletter for the Federal Reserve Bank of St. Louis.

A few economists, such as Benjamin Reed Shiller at Brandeis University, have been studying what might happen if firms know everything about you. In a 2013 academic paper, Shiller looked at Netflix, structuring a model to see what happens to profits when Netflix collects various degrees of information about its customers. Just having basic demographic information alone to offer different prices increases profits 0.14 percent. Adding data from web-browsing history increases profits 1.4 percent, with some customers paying twice as much for the same product as others. This is just the tip of the iceberg. The potential for companies to make consumers pay more is enormous.

Dynamic pricing is not going away, nor is price discrimination. With every advance in technology, dynamic pricing gets more sophisticated and cheaper for companies to use. As a result, business profits have fattened. Without any laws to protect consumers, and with most of the economics profession telling policy makers to back off, consumers are on their own. Every single purchase will be a contest against a seller who knows a tremendous amount about the buyer. It's pretty clear who the odds favor. But consumers will also be pitted against every other consumer in seeking the best deal. English philosopher Herbert Spencer, after reading Charles Darwin's theory of natural selection, coined the phrase "survival of the fittest." The phrase may be just as appropriate for commerce in the digital age. The predators atop the food chain aren't going to object.

5

Everything Tailored to You

On Friday, December 4, 2009, Google technicians wrote an enthusiastic blog post about a change to Google Search. For the first time, Google Search would be personalized for every single user on the planet. It was as if Google had suddenly flipped a switch. One day, search was the same for everyone; the next it was tailored to who you were and what Google knew about you.

Although Google's roll out of personalization for all happened almost overnight, in reality it had been evolving for years. Since the start of the company back in 1998, founders Sergey Brin and Larry Page, as well as their chief of technology, Craig Silverstein, dreamed aloud of developing a perfect search algorithm. Their notion of perfect always incorporated an element of adapting to the user. Because every person is unique, search needed to respond to each and every person individually. That technological challenge remained out of reach in the early days of search. But once Google began to dominate other search engines by figuring out how best to respond to most people, it focused on extending its technological lead even more. Personalization became a priority.

Within Google, Silverstein directed the development of personalized search at Google Labs, where the company developed and, more importantly, tested new products and services on their users in the public realm. Interested and engaged Google users could play around with Google's latest public ideas and provide critical feedback to the company's engineers (the program was shut down in 2011). On March 29, 2004, Google launched its test version of personalized search. In the beginning Google approached personalization very differently from other companies like Amazon and Microsoft, which were trying to solve similar problems at the time. Its competitors learned everything they could about their users and then made assumptions. Google thought it could create personalized search by asking users about themselves.

Google's first version of personalized search asked users to check various categories about themselves to help make their search process faster. It was a pretty crude system. The categories covered interests like sports and entertainment and the questions were simple and standard. So if a user checked tennis as an interest, when searching for balls she would immediately see tennis balls because Google knew they were relevant to her interests.

In an interview posted online around the time of the test launch, Silverstein defended Google's approach over its competitors. "In the latter [competitor's] scenario, where first you learn, and then you help the visitor out, you have two places where the computer has to make intelligent judgments," he said. "I am not saying that it's not an interesting or promising approach, but it does put more strain on the computer. When you tell it what your interests are, then the computer only has to be intelligent to use that information to try to help you out. They are both part of the same goal of trying to help people out with personal information—it is just a matter of how you get there. We will be seeing more of this in the future."

Months later, Google changed its approach. Relying on users to provide accurate information proved not as effective as gathering that information independently from users. Because Google was the leading aggregator of information in the world, that seemed a practical option. By late 2005 the test days of personalized search ended. Google incorporated personalized search as a normal part of search for users with Google accounts like Gmail, Blogger, YouTube, or Google Groups. For anyone who signed up for one or more of Google's services, Google could easily create a profile to serve as the basis for customizing his or her search results. At the time, personalized Google Search covered hundreds of millions of people around the world—anyone with a Gmail or YouTube account, for instance.

Google's personalized search remained exclusive to account holders for four years. Then in December 2009 Google changed its search algorithm to provide personalization for all users. By planting cookies on a search user's computer, Google began remembering searches and tracking web-surfing histories. Together with all its other sources of data, Google could create a detailed profile of each user tied to the cookies and other unique identifiers. Each profile then became a template for tailoring search to the relevant individual. Today Google's personalized search is not just based on your web history but can access everything the company knows about you: where you live, who your friends are, who you work for, your likes and interests, your interactions on social-networking sites, what you buy, and so on. And there's no way to turn back the clock. Personalized search cannot be completely removed from your Google Search. That means there's no standard or typical set of results for a search. Every person who searches for tennis balls, for instance, may get slightly (or dramatically) different results based on gender, age, income, social groups, and location, among other things. One person's query for news about politics, say, may return different results than a neighbor or a friend's query.

In 2012 DuckDuckGo, an emerging search engine and competitor to Google, ran a series of experiments on Google Search. DuckDuck-Go's founder, Gabriel Weinberg, developed the search engine for users who didn't want to be tracked or didn't want to see the Internet through tailor-made glasses. The experiments showed that no matter what they did, every web search on Google was personalized. "I didn't expect so much variation for signed out US users," Weinberg was reported to have said on TPM, a digital-news website. "You expect some personalization when you're signed in. But if you're signed out or in incognito mode, you expect to get the 'regular results.' What we found is there are no more 'regular results' on Google."

Much has been made about the social and political implications of personalized search. Eli Pariser's brilliant 2011 book *The Filter Bubble* revealed the negative side of personalized search. Up to that point, Google and other companies freely touted personalized search as great for the public because it made search faster and more efficient. Personalized search is more likely to show people what they want to see than a generic search result. But Pariser explained that all that increased efficiency comes with a cost. It tends to divide society into like-minded people, cut off from other perspectives and views. As a result, it could undermine the very existence of our democracy. Pariser worried that in the end, personalized search led in one direction: to reduce creativity and to limit intellectual challenges by reinforcing biases and prejudices. So instead of expanding our human intelligence, in an ironic twist, personalized search may actually in some ways contract it.

Pariser raised important questions about the social and political implications of personalized search. But there are profound commercial implications too. Personalization of search begins with advertising. The more advertising that companies like Google, Facebook, and Amazon can sell, the more money they make. So at its crudest, personalized search is a way to sell more advertising. More importantly, it's about selling more expensive advertising. The more targeted the ad, the more Google can charge. And the more effective the ad is in enticing consumers to click on it, the more companies like Google can get paid. Advertising in itself is not bad for consumers. In theory, advertising can benefit consumers by making them aware of their option to buy a product or service. Nobody has to buy something just because he or she sees an ad. But the commercial and economic effects of personalized search and advertising can be insidious. First off, companies can reap huge rewards from personalization. After all, personalization is a means to get at the consumer surplus. And by determining what consumers see, web companies are excellently positioned to influence buying decisions. That kind of power is extremely valuable.

Personalized search leads to personalized advertising and then to personalized websites. The whole experience of the Internet can be customized to each user. Websites that remember our locations and previous purchases can recommend products just for us at special prices. There's no incentive to save consumers money. In fact, the incentives tend in the other direction.

But personalization is not isolated to the virtual world. New technologies are spreading personalization throughout the offline, brick-and-mortar world as well. For years now, services have tended to be highly personalized. Think of hiring a gardener or a housekeeper. You require specific things unique to you and your house or garden and negotiate a price. Up until recently, personalized products have tended to be rare because they were inefficient to manufacture. But with new technology, personalization is sweeping through product markets too. As more and more of what you see and buy is tailored to you, your relationship with sellers and to the market is changing. And that has important implications for each one of us.

If Google had never crossed the line to sell advertising, personalized search would be very different today. So would users' relationship with the company. When search results are directly tied to advertising dollars, as Google's are, the personalization of search has a real economic impact for the consumer. Google can determine what you see and what you don't see when you search. That means the company has a big say in your economic choices—what you buy and how much you spend.

In Google's early days, it had no advertising. Between 1998 and 2000, the company was all about organizing information on the web to help users find what they were looking for. Its page rankings were determined by the most relevant sites or the sites people clicked on most. By the end of 1998, Google had indexed about 60 million pages and was developing a following because of a sleek and simple design and results that seemed to be better than the other search engines at that time.

It wasn't until 2000 that Google began selling advertising. It happened without much fanfare through the launch of Adwords in October of that year. Through Adwords, Google sold advertising associated with keywords in search. Advertisers paid a price based on the number of clicks per ad. Suddenly, Google's priorities changed. Instead of providing search users with neutral tools to decide what they should click on, the company had some skin in the game. For the first time, Google had a real economic incentive to get users to click on some things rather than others. That marked the start of an uneasy relationship between Google and its users that continues today. On the one hand, Google has to satisfy advertisers that pay for its services. On the other, it has to maintain trust with users so they continue to use Google. Without either one, Google would be history.

Google founders Brin and Page have always known that incorporating advertising into search is detrimental to users. In a 1998 research paper called *The Anatomy of a Large-Scale Hypertextual Web Search Engine*, the pair wrote: "(We) expect that advertising funded search engines will be inherently biased towards the advertisers and away from the needs of consumers." As every user is also a consumer, a search driven by advertising fundamentally changes the relationship between Google and its users. Prior to selling advertising, Google worked for users. It focused solely on doing the best job for its users; so for instance, if someone searched for a person's name, the engine would turn up results from a reliable web source for free. Once the company sold advertising, though, it had an incentive to find that person's name on a site requiring you to pay for it—preferably one that paid Google for advertising.

An equities analyst at Trefis explains clearly how Google gets paid for what it does. According to the analyst: "Advertisers on Google bid for keywords (such as 'NYC restaurants') to display their advertisements on the Google search page. Google AdWords allows these advertisers to display advertisements in Google's search results and the Google Content Network through either a cost-per-click or cost-per-view scheme. The pricing of keywords, the inventory of keywords available, and the frequency of user search, impact how much money Google makes on search." In addition, Google makes money by placing ads on its other services, such as Gmail and YouTube, as well as placing ads on its partner websites through AdSense.

Google shows you things it wants you to click on. That's how it makes money. The more you click, the more money it makes. For the advertisers, the most valuable clicks are the ones that bring the biggest profits. There's a direct conflict of interest involved. Google does better financially when it guides you to a seller that charges more rather than less. But if you find out, you might stop trusting Google, so the less Google explains itself, the better. Meanwhile, Google has an incentive not simply to show you things but to sell you things. And that means that in October 2000, when Google started selling advertising, it stopped being an information aggregator on behalf of users and became just another seller.

Customizing Our Every Click

Search has been at the forefront of personalizing our Internet experience. Now every website follows the trend. Today your entire experience, from search to site, is tailored to you. The idea is not necessarily to sell you more stuff but to sell you more expensive stuff. Tailoring products and services allows companies to charge higher prices than for mass-market goods.

For some time now, the mighty online retailer Amazon has customized its website, but custom websites are now one of the hottest trends in marketing. From small to large, web-marketing companies like Marketo, HubSpot, and Pardot offer ways to personalize the experience of visiting a website, the explicit rationale being that the more relevant a site is to a consumer, the more likely it is that he or she will spend money. So far, website customization is still pretty trivial. You might go to the Citibank website for your online banking and see an ad for Coke while another person sees an ad for Pepsi. Or, a website will allow personalized account settings so users can change displays and color schemes and choose favorite settings. Sometimes it's annoying. You might have noticed advertisements that pop up for similar products you have just bought online. In that case, you have to wonder what they're thinking. Once you buy each of your children a specific backpack for the new school year, are you really going to buy another?

Then there are the more sophisticated customizations in which a site captures your information, preferences, and history and dynamically changes what it shows you. This so-called *dynamic website personalization*, in which sites change the content, messaging, products, and services displayed to an individual visitor based on his or her web behavior, personal history, and location, is where all websites are heading right now.

To date, Amazon has set the standard for big online retailers who customize their websites. When you click on Amazon's site, the first things that appear in the corner are your name and product recommendations based on products you bought in the past, products you've viewed, and ratings as well as a range of personal details Amazon has gathered about you. The more an Amazon customer shops on the site, the more the website's content is personalized. In a paper published in 2003, Amazon described how it is able to provide personalized recommendations:

> Amazon.com extensively uses recommendation algorithms to personalize its Web site to each customer's interests. Because existing recommendation algorithms cannot scale to Amazon.com's tens of millions of customers and products, we developed our own. Our algorithm, item-to-item collaborative filtering, scales to massive data sets and produces high-quality recommendations in real time . . . Rather than matching the user to similar customers, item-to-item collaborative filtering matches each of the user's purchased and rated items to similar items, then combines those similar items into a recommendation list. To determine the most-similar match for a given item, the algorithm builds a similar-items table by finding items that customers tend to purchase together.

In order to customize its web content and make individual product suggestions, Amazon.com uses cookies. Cookies are essentially identification tags that websites store on your computer when you first visit the site. That allows the website to track you and remember what you do on the site, from clicking on links to turning pages and filling out any information. They also record how long you stay on the website, your personal preferences, and what items you buy. Cookies ensure that the next time you visit the site, all that information is remembered. Nearly all websites these days use cookies and may alert visitors to that fact. Because basic cookies can be deleted, making it impossible for advertisers to track web users, new types of cookies like flash or evercookies have been invented, which are harder to delete and allow sites to keep tracking you. Evercookies, for instance, continuously copy themselves on an individual website and therefore cannot easily be deleted.

Netflix is another example of online customization with which many of us are familiar. Users receive film recommendations based on what they have previously watched. The company also has a "personalize" option where you answer questions about different genres and rate shows and movies you've seen. Once you watch something, you can hit a recommend button or share your reaction with friends on Facebook.

Netflix gives its users the option to identify their interests within the site. Other websites provide customization on a similar basis. For instance, content on an online educational site can change according to whether you identify yourself as a teacher, parent, or student. Or think of a job website—what you see depends on whether you're looking for a job or trying to fill a position. Most websites, though, track your browsing history and the search terms you used to get to the site to personalize the content. Although the trend of customizing the Internet is, in many ways, still pretty crude, it is evolving rapidly. In marketing- and management-consulting circles, a lot of energy is currently going into developing and exploiting this new frontier. Just think about the untapped potential with regard to advertising. How long before advertisers show you images and ads that cater to racial stereotypes or socioeconomic status? What about if they know you favor a certain look and disapprove of another, say, someone with lots of tattoos and body piercings? How easy then might it be to cast the competition in a bad light and their own products in a good light by using different looks for people in the ads? And if you can only see what's shown to you, who's to know what everyone else sees? Think of how a new breakfast cereal could advertise and appeal to each one of us successfully. Every cereal these days has many different variations. For instance, My Muesli offers eighty different ingredients you can use to customize your own product.

My Muesli is a great example of how the online and offline world have merged. When you buy from the company, you're buying physical, edible muesli, but you never enter a shop. You choose your ingredients and even the packaging, like eat-on-the-go containers, and it's all done online. No company can operate without a significant online capability these days. As Devin Wenig, the president of eBay Marketplaces, told McKinsey & Company in an interview in 2014: "I think e-commerce for many years was an interesting trend, but it was on the side, largely, of what was happening in retail. Today we don't even know what e-commerce means. They've just come together, the on- and the offline. Now, every merchant, every retailer must have an omnichannel strategy or they won't survive. That's very different than even just 24 months ago." And the flow isn't all one way, either. Online companies are developing offline presence as well. For instance, Amazon has been considering opening a mini warehouse with capabilities for returns and order pickups at its 34th Street office building in Manhattan.

From Search to Shirts: The Spread of Mass Customization

Web personalization is facilitating the spread of customization throughout the economy and vice versa. And that means Google's personalized search is really part of a bigger trend in the economy, the trend from mass markets to mass customization. In marketing, manufacturing, and services, mass customization is spreading quickly. In essence, mass customization means the tailoring of advertisements, content, products, and services to an individual's desires, in real time and cost effectively, with the use of technology. McKinsey says that the era of mass customization has finally arrived, thanks to new technologies, and the management consultant expects mass customization to deliver bigger profits for companies. Today many companies offer customized products, including apparel such as sneakers, shirts, and suits; food such as coffee, tea, and muesli; health and beauty products such as vitamins and cosmetics; and recreational goods such as golf clubs, bicycles, and garden design. Even companies that have embraced a one-size-fits-all approach to their businesses are now adopting customization. Think of JetBlue, for example.

When the low-cost airline was first launched in 1999, it promised a better and more people-friendly flying experience for everyone. A key difference was that every seat was more or less the same, offering better legroom than other airlines without making the usual distinction of economy, business, and first class. Everyone who flew JetBlue essentially flew budget class. It was a classic mass-market idea of air travel, and in a way it was a retro approach, an effort to, perhaps intentionally, re-create the atmosphere of flying in the good old days when it was glamorous and exciting—before airlines began to treat everyone, particularly economy-class fliers, like cattle.

But without segmenting its customers, JetBlue left a lot of the consumer surplus on the table. It missed out on those customers who would pay up to fly at the front of the aircraft in nicer seats with more attentive service or who wanted more legroom. So in 2008 Jet-Blue began offering customers a choice: They could pay up for extra legroom. The airline also introduced a number of other optional services at the same time, such as a fifteen-dollar charge for a second checked bag. JetBlue calculated at the time that the measures would increase its revenue by about $60 million a year; $40 million from allowing customers to choose more legroom and $20 million from checked-luggage fees. Then starting in 2014, JetBlue introduced its Mint seats. These are premium seats at the front of the plane on transcontinental flights that are more expensive than regular budget seats or extended-legroom seats. A Mint seat entitles a customer to a fully flat seat, fresher food, priority check-in and boarding, and faster baggage claim. In other words, Mint is essentially the same thing as the premium class offered by other airlines.

Although JetBlue began with a standard product for all some fifteen years or so ago, it wasn't long before it began to segment its market. To be fair, JetBlue was simply following what every other airline has done. Think of the introduction of premium economy seating in recent years, for instance, dividing economy into two segments and charging more for a little extra legroom. With online booking, airlines can segment their customers even more. By giving air travelers more choices about the size of seats, the location of seats, the number of checked bags, types of entertainment, different foods, different flying routes, the number of stops, and all sorts of other conveniences and services, airlines can create a unique product for each one of their customers. It's amazing how far we've come from the idea that we're all flying on the same plane. And that means airlines can charge each customer a unique price. Customization is occurring in large and small ways throughout the economy. Some companies offer consumers the chance to create a unique product. An example is the men's online suit maker Indochino. It shows you how to take your measurements, promising it will take only ten minutes, and then you choose the style, fabric, and all the small details to create a custom-made suit, delivered in four weeks. Other companies like Land's End offer smaller custom details such as monograms on bags or names on backpacks. A small garment maker, Wild Thing, allows customers to choose between three different jacket types, colors, and fabrics with some discretion on styling for pockets and hoods. Food companies have also been offering personalized products. Tea maker Adagio allows customers to choose between many different types of loose-leaf teas to create their own unique combinations. Another type of customization is through product bundling— choosing standard products but in a combination or a bundle that is unique to the shopper, such as a gift basket.

In a 2013 report, management consultant firm Bain and Co. conducted a survey and found that consumers were willing to pay far more for customized products. Bain partners Elizabeth Spaulding and Christopher Perry wrote in the brief: "We found that customers are willing to pay 20% more than standard equivalents for customized products—and many companies are successfully charging higher premiums." McKinsey and Bain are so excited about mass customization because it is highly profitable for companies. Further in the article they quote Ken Seiff, executive vice president of direct and omnichannel marketing at Brooks Brothers, who says, "In general, customers who buy customized products are more satisfied and are more valuable. By automating customization using the Web, companies can more easily take a customer segment down to the size of one. In five years this will come to be expected by consumers." Seiff's comments are revealing and highlight the higher profitability of customization. His comments point to where we are heading, with market segments made up of each individual customer, and underscore the inevitability of the trend. Without doubt, mass customization is here to stay and will become highly sophisticated.

Mass customization is not entirely a new idea. For the past two decades at least, management consultants have identified the great business opportunities rising from personalizing products and services. Although consumers and companies have been keen on the idea, technology has lagged. Today that has changed, and many new technologies are speeding up the ability of mass customization to sweep across industries. Implementing mass customization in manufacturing in particular has been challenging and limited without the rise of new technological tools. But a number of developments have enabled the mass customization of manufactured products. In the 1990s manufacturers moved to just-in-time inventory, which relied on a flexible and lean method of production pioneered by the auto industry. Toyota, in fact, established lean manufacturing and flexible production, which GM and Ford Motor Company eventually followed, influencing other manufacturers like Caterpillar and computer makers like Dell. Without flexible manufacturing systems, customization would be costly. It allows manufacturers to switch almost instantly between models and types with little disruption to the production process. Software to help companies manage their supply chains is also making the manufacturing process far more predictable with regard to customization. According to a 2014 McKinsey research article on the topic: "The time for widespread, profitable mass customization may finally have come, the result of emerging or improved technologies that can help address economic barriers to responding to consumers' exact needs in a more precise way."

Perhaps the most important new technology enabling mass customization is 3-D printing. Think of it as an industrial robot that can weld, paint, assemble, pick up, and place material together precisely. 3-D printing makes three-dimensional objects out of metal, ceramics, fabrics, and edible materials like chocolate. It works by first making a 3-D digital design of a product. The design is then put into a modeling program that essentially slices the product into hundreds and thousands of thin layers. When the 3-D printer begins to print, it replicates each one of the thin slices to make one three-dimensional product. The technology was developed in the 1980s but was most often used for building prototypes of products. Now, however, many different industries incorporate 3-D printing into their production processes, including the automotive, aerospace, dental, medical, and even food industries. Some products made using 3-D printers include bikes, cars, clothing, jewelry, furniture, and home decorations.

At a 3-D printing show in London in September 2014, Strakka Racing unveiled a new car built with parts made by 3-D printing. "It's not uncommon to use 3D printing for rapid prototyping, which helps a very short development cycle, but what we've moved into now is actual production parts on a race car, which is quite a new direction for us to go," Dan Walmsley, an engineer at Strakka Racing, told reporters at the time. "We found that the material properties have recently moved forward to a point where they're stiff enough and strong enough and light enough to function as a fully finished production component on a race car." Another example is Shapeways, a New York–based company that uses 3-D printing to make custom home items, jewelry, games, and other items. A customer can create his or her own ring online by choosing the basic shape, metals, design, and engravings. A vase can be customized by submitting text that is then shown as an image, created by a 3-D printer, and sent to the customer a few days later. According to McKinsey, "The advances of this technology mean that the primary constraint in adoption will be the creativity of entrepreneurs and leaders in how it is applied. As mind-sets about what is possible change, we expect many more innovative concepts and processes to blossom that accelerate the cost-effective production of customized goods." Experts predict 3-D printing will spread mass customization throughout the manufacturing sector, especially as it becomes cheaper and more sophisticated. According to a 2013 *New York Times* article, the price of 3-D printers dropped dramatically from 2011 to 2013, from $20,000 to $1,000 or so.

Other technologies are helping to spread mass customization. "Recommendation engines are now moving into the customization space by helping customers configure products," according to an article by McKinsey. Chocri, a Germany-based chocolate maker, lets customers create their own chocolate bars online. It recently expanded into the United States. Customers can choose from four different chocolate bases and one hundred different toppings to create their own sweet treats. But the website's real genius is the use of recommendation technology to help customers determine whether their topping choices actually make a delicious, or not-so-delicious, combination. "Recommendations are based on popular choices users of the site have made and are edited by the company for taste, thereby reducing the risk the customer takes when ordering a product she or he has never tasted. Chocri estimates that its recommendation engine has increased the rate of conversion from people configuring their own chocolate to an actual online order by more than 30 percent," wrote McKinsey. The more a website knows about you, the more it can tailor products to you and make recommendations. And don't we like having a helpful and attentive shop assistant when we are shopping? Only this one will know a lot more about us than if we had just walked in off the street.

The Dark Side of Customization

Customization is pushing into every aspect of our world as consumers. Both online and offline, advertising, products, and services are being tailored to each one of us. So what are the implications? For starters, customization should reward consumers, right? After all, it's about every single one of us getting a pair of shoes or jeans that fits exactly. Customization in itself is not bad for consumers. It should mean more choices and getting what we really want at prices that we can afford to pay. And that's an awesome development in consumer markets. Who would ever have thought that customized suits, something that only a rarified few could purchase in the past, would be affordable to the middle class? So customization has a great potential to be positive for consumers. The trouble is there's also a negative side to customization.

Although customization may allow you to get what you want, it won't allow you to easily trade what you get if you tire of it or need money. When you purchase a pair of shoes tailored especially for you, it's not easy to find someone exactly like you to trade with should you decide you don't need them after all. Who wants shoes that have been made to fit you? It's not impossible, but the more customized the product, the more limited the resale market. You can see this principle at work in terms of housing. The more unique the color of the walls, carpets, and bathrooms, the harder a house is to sell. So real-estate brokers often encourage buyers to use neutral colors throughout to get the best price.

Then there's price transparency. With customized products and services, you can't see if you're getting a fair price. All you can see is what you're being charged for a unique product. How can you compare prices when every product is unique? Customization is part of the intentional destruction of the mass market. Customization makes everything different and nothing comparable. As soon as it's not comparable, you can't be sure what you're paying is fair.

Personalized advertising plays a role in obscuring price too. Once Google sold advertising, it became a middleman connecting buyers and sellers and charging a fee for that service. In that role it has replaced the newspapers that were the old-school middlemen. Newspapers had their own balancing act, trying to satisfy the interests of advertisers, owners, and readers. They were terrifically profitable and important. But Google is many times bigger, both in its financial muscle as well as its reach. Google's reach in promoting personalized advertising is having a different effect from the mass-market advertising found in newspapers, for instance. When a reader of the *New York Times* sees an advertisement for Chopard diamonds for $10,000, it's like seeing a stock-market quote. That reader knows where the market is for high-end diamonds. Whether he ever wants to buy high-end diamonds is another matter—but at least he has a little piece of data to file away for another time. It's the same principle when the *New York Times* advertises sheet sets at Macy's for $89.99 or the latest Michael Kors dress at Saks Fifth Avenue for $499.00. A micro ad pitched to an individual Google user does not carry the same market information. You see a price for you, but you don't know whether it's the same or different from others. So micromarket advertising or custom ads differ in two ways from regular mass-market ads. First, you may be getting a special deal tailored to you. Second, you don't take away any knowledge about what others are paying.

Not only does mass customization make the market price more opaque but it also takes our focus off price and puts it onto our wants and desires. Think about how it works. Instead of going to the store and asking about what products are available and at what price, the flow of information is just the opposite. The store asks you, the consumer, what you want. You can't customize unless you first ask customers what their desires are. Once a transaction is based on your wants, not what things cost, sellers can charge a lot more. So with mass customization, the consumer's fundamental focus shifts from price to want. And when you want something, you're more likely to pay up for it. That's partly why a firm like McKinsey believes mass customization is very profitable for companies. It changes the equation from customers asking, "What have you got and how much does it cost?" to customers revealing what they want and how much they're willing to pay.

Price is an important factor we consider that helps shape our wants and at times can actually change them. When you find out that a new Audi with all the customized bells and whistles comes to $80,000— far more than you wanted to pay—it may change your desire for a new Audi. Perhaps, you might rather have a used Audi with low mileage for one-third the price. But if you're not offered the used Audi at one-third the price, then you may be locked into paying for the higher-priced Audi or you may switch to a different brand that you like less. When everything is tailored to you, including search, sites, products, and services, you're not seeing what's truly available in the marketplace. You're seeing what's available to you. The mass-market paradigm is one in which you reveal nothing, and you get to look at a tremendous variety of options and know that you're seeing the real price that everyone else is seeing. Price is printed on the aisle. But that paradigm is disappearing. Loyalty cards, discounts, and club memberships are all ways of obscuring the price.

Even more importantly, when we are offered both products and information tailored just for us, it may seem like a benefit, but in fact we give up some of our own autonomy to the tailor. Because what we want is related to what we are shown, anybody in the business of showing us what we want is in a powerful position because, in effect, they can tell us what we want. That's especially true when they know us better than we know ourselves.

When you walk into a store, you can see everything that's on the shelf and make a decision. When you search for tennis racquets and see only high-end racquets, are you really getting more choice? Just like Pariser's idea of the filter bubble—that personalized search may make us dumber, not smarter—mightn't personalized search have the same unintended consequence for the consumer? Instead of more choice, might we end up with less? As Google strives for efficiency, why would it show us a range of tennis racquets when it knows we can afford an expensive brand? A tennis racquet is pretty trivial in the scheme of things, but if everything we search for is cut down to products and services Google guesses we will like, doesn't that take away our ability to choose? Mightn't we want the freedom to see the entire product range and make a decision? So the great irony of personalized search, and everything that goes with it, is that it may, in fact, restrict our choices in the marketplace rather than increase them. Instead of walking into a store, seeing what's available, and looking at the price tag, your experience online will boil down to walking into a store and being asked how much you want to spend. Once you tell the storekeeper what you want to spend, you'll only be shown products in that category.

Dividing consumers into tailored segments also exacerbates the social and political divide. If you only see and buy an eight-dollar Coke and I only see and buy a one-dollar Coke, we don't inhabit the same world. Furthermore, segmentation negatively affects the quality of lower-priced products and services. Sellers have no incentive to produce high-quality, low-priced goods and services. They want many people to step up and pay for the next level of product and service. Think of airlines in this regard. These days it's easy to believe that most airlines make flying economy about as miserable an experience as possible so that those who can afford it will travel premium or business class.

Mass customization also affects the knowledge gap. Personalization is about knowing more and more about you. The more you tell sellers what you want, the more intimately they know you. So personalization makes the knowledge gap bigger, and that exacerbates the imbalance of power in the market between you and the seller. Google describes its customization of search as making it easier for its users to get what they want. But customization allows companies to charge different prices for very small variations in the same product or service. We think we're getting exactly what we want when someone makes us a customized product, but in the process, they're actually learning the maximum price we're willing to pay.

Customization is about a fundamental change in the marketplace. Instead of many buyers and sellers for a product or service, there's one seller and one buyer. It's you up against Citibank, GM, or Amazon with all their financial resources and knowledge of you and the marketplace. There's no standard price anymore, and that means there's a price and product tailored to you. Without a market price, the free market as we know it will cease to exist.

The more information sellers have about you, the finer the distinctions they can make and, ultimately, the better they are at setting individualized prices according to the most they expect you'd be willing to pay. So customization of the web leads in one direction: to allow companies to extract as much of the consumer surplus as possible. There may be some payoff to consumers in the form of getting what you want. But how will you know if you're really getting what you want or if you're getting what sellers want you to have? The potential to control your buying habits is enormous.

Together with price discrimination, mass customization is reshaping our economy. But those are not the only tools companies have to extract the consumer surplus. Price discrimination and mass customization are major tools that are becoming widely used, but companies nibble away at the surplus in many smaller ways. Putting all the tools together, companies are in an unstoppable position to extract our wealth on a vast scale.

6

The Proliferation of Fine Print

A **little button to the side** of an article you're reading about health and wellness on the Mayo Clinic website catches your eye: Lose up to six to ten pounds in two weeks by following the Mayo Clinic diet, based on the *New York Times* best-selling book. It's intriguing. After all, you've wanted to lose ten pounds for a while now and nothing seems to work. If anyone should have good advice on diets, it should be the Mayo Clinic. It's one of the leading medical authorities in the world.

So you click the button. What the heck, it can't hurt, and you may learn something useful. Next you wind up on a page where you can get your "free diet profile." Big letters across the screen promise "the last diet you'll ever need." All you have to do is fill out your age, weight, and height and answer a few questions. You know that selling diets is like selling snake oil but come on, this is the Mayo Clinic. It's among the most respected hospitals and medical care facilities in the United States. The Mayo Clinic brand is all about looking after people. If anyone has a diet program that isn't just another rip-off, it ought to be the Mayo Clinic.

Trusting the Mayo Clinic's reputation, you enter your personal information and click through the prompts. A series of questions appear before you can go any further. Do you ever watch TV while eating? What do you consider a serving size of pasta? The size of a hockey puck? Tennis ball? Or softball? What's your biggest motivation to lose weight? Family? Health? An upcoming event? To look better? How active are you? What activities do you do? What's the biggest obstacle to you losing weight right now? What health topics interest you right now? Based on your answers, the Mayo Clinic then recommends different types of newsletters that they produce and you can receive via e-mail. In order to go on, you have to sign up to receive them before you can create your "free diet profile."

So you sign up for one or two newsletters. It's free, right? Then you hit the button to create your profile. If you were hoping to find some answers, you're disappointed. More marketing material appears about what you can learn from the Mayo Clinic diet, which has five main points: break bad habits, adjust food portions, look and feel your best, overcome emotional eating, and receive support from Mayo Clinic experts. All true, perhaps, but not what you expected. You thought you would get some specific ideas on how to lose weight. What does a diet profile mean, anyway? It's vague enough that it might imply a lot of different things. But not to worry. An orange button near the bottom of the page says Start Losing Weight. All you have to do is click on it.

Click on it and it takes you to a new page where you have to start an account and provide a credit card so that you can start losing weight today. "Join now and get your first 7 days free," and in smaller print, "Just $4/week after that." Well, you hadn't expected to pay for anything. It did say free. But then you can always try it for seven days and cancel after that, right? You might get some really good ideas for losing weight and then you really won't ever have to diet again. You enter your e-mail address and credit-card information. At the bottom of the page is a big button with a red Sign Up Now. Just on top in small print is the sentence, "By signing up you agree to the terms of service and billing policy." And to reassure you that they take your privacy seriously is an image of a padlock with Comodo Secure written next to it.

If you read the fine print, you might think twice before signing up. But then, who has the time or the patience to read through the fine print? Most of it is legalese, anyway. But the fine print actually is informative for what it includes as well as what it doesn't include. Perhaps the most interesting aspect is that even after reading the fine print, you can't be sure of what you are getting. The only way to know is to sign up. The site actually makes no promises. It alludes to a personal diet plan, but is that really what you get? And without any extra costs? It won't say. There's a sidebar that lists many enticing things: "Get All the Tools You Need to Lose Weight: personalized meal plans, 100s of easy delicious recipes, simple portion control guides, motivational tips, healthy habit tracker, food and fitness journal, vitamin and nutrient log, personalized workouts, exercise guides and videos, walking and running guides." Wow! That's a lot of things, and it seems like by signing up that's exactly what you'll get. But it never explicitly says that. Do you really get everything you will need at no extra charge? That's hard to believe, and yet it's written to entice you into believing it. The bottom line is that there's no way of knowing what you get until you give the Mayo Clinic your credit-card information.

What becomes clear from reading the fine print is that your costs might easily be more than you expect. Look carefully at what the Mayo Clinic writes in the fine print about the Mayo Clinic diet:

The Mayo Clinic Diet's online program is yours FREE for 7 days! You will not be charged during your free trial period. However, valid payment information is required. If you're happy with your online membership, do nothing. Your service will continue uninterrupted, and you will be enrolled under our standard membership agreement. Online membership is just $4 a week, billed in advance quarterly (every 13 weeks). The charge will be applied to the same account you provide at sign-up. You may cancel before your free trial ends at no charge, or at any time afterward and you will continue to have access to your account for the remainder of your term.

First, don't forget, this was advertised as a two-week program. So any decision to end it in seven days will probably not deliver the results you were looking for. Second, how do you cancel it? There's nothing that says exactly how you go about canceling. And that's not uncommon these days. Websites can make it difficult to cancel a customer agreement although signing up is quite easy. Some go to extreme lengths, and you have to first find a phone number that is not easily found on the website. You might be placed on hold for what seems like ages before a representative will speak with you. And in many cases you are quizzed about why you want to terminate the relationship. It's not like the Mayo Clinic tells you how to cancel in its fine print. It could easily state, "You may cancel by pressing this big red button." If the Mayo Clinic is really serious about giving you a diet that works, why doesn't it let you sign up for seven days and then ask you to pay? If you love the program, why wouldn't you pay? But on the other hand, if you sign up and are not impressed, you may very well forget or be too busy to cancel. Gotcha! Your free trial might not be free after all.

Even customers who like the product may pay more than they think and use less of the product. The advertised price is four dollars a week. But customers pay for thirteen weeks at a time, in fifty-two dollar chunks. That gives you thirteen weeks of the "program," although you still don't know what it is. And remember, the original come-on said you can lose weight in two weeks. There's no useful explanation of what you get for the money or during the "free" trial period. You have to pay in full for it, and if you want to cancel at any time during that thirteen-week period, you don't get your money back. You do, however, get to keep using a service you're not happy with and want to cancel until the thirteen weeks are up.

What about the even-finer print: the terms of service and the privacy policy that require clicking and scrolling through a number of legal points. As a hospital, the Mayo Clinic can't just pass your health information on to third parties. But as a website service trading on the reputation the Mayo Clinic has built up over years, it can pass on information it collects from you to anyone it decides to. First look at the terms of service. When you boil it all down, the policy says you agree to pay and have limited rights, and the website can change its policies if it wants. Then there's the privacy policy. In terms of sharing your information, the website says it can disclose personal information for legal reasons and to agents and contractors as well as to businesses associated with the website:

> We may provide your Personal Information to service providers who work on our behalf or help us to operate our business, the Site and the Services. Examples of such service providers include vendors and suppliers that provide us with technology, services, and/or content for sending email, analyzing data, research, providing advertising and marketing assistance, processing payments (including credit card payments), and providing customer service. Access to your Personal Information by these service providers is limited to the information reasonably necessary to perform its limited function.

Whatever "reasonably necessary" means! That's a lot of different companies with access to your personal information. But the bigger issue is what it terms "anonymous information." There are no restrictions on sharing anonymous information. The difference between personal information and anonymous information is simple: It's anonymous if it can't be "reasonably" tied back to an individual person. That's a huge loophole. The cookies that companies stash on your browser don't identify you. They identify your browser. So the website can take the most sensitive and personal information it has and sell it to third parties along with the cookie data. Online, nobody needs to know your name. You show up online as a browser with cookies. And companies can use your personal data, linked to your computer through cookies, however they want.

Another thing to keep in mind is that there's no longer any such thing as anonymous information. With the help of reidentification techniques, a large portion of online data can be traced back to individuals. And if all that isn't enough, the website can change its policies and practices at any time without notice, and the changes will become effective immediately:

> We reserve the right to change, modify, add or remove portions of this Policy at any time and without prior notice, and any changes will become effective immediately upon being posted unless we advise you otherwise. Your continued use of the Site or Services after this Policy has been amended shall be deemed to be your continued acceptance of the terms and conditions of the Policy, as amended. We encourage you to bookmark this Web page and review this Policy regularly.

The website helpfully recommends you spend your time monitoring its user policy for any changes that might be important to you. That's a patently absurd suggestion. It would be a rare user who even reads enough of the policy to find the suggestion that he or she check back frequently. This is a diet-advice site, for heaven's sake. Anybody who carefully monitors the fine print on a diet site in case it changes doesn't need diet advice. Psychiatric help seems more appropriate. It's clear that all the fine print was prepared by lawyers to protect the website. It's not a real contract, in the sense that both parties understand what they are agreeing to. It's a one-sided deal that typically is not even read by the consumer. The only time it will be referred to is if a

120 **ALL YOU CAN PAY**

problem arises later, in which case the website will pull out the policy and use it as a first line of defense, claiming that the customer agreed to its terms and that it is absolved from responsibility.

Step back for a moment to understand what the website has done. It has created a valuable list of the names and the e-mails of people who want to lose weight. Even if the website doesn't sell that list to third parties, it has a rich source of prospects to whom it can sell future diet products and services. And if it doesn't want to hand over the list, it can serve as a middleman between companies who want to market to weight-loss customers and the valuable list of prospects. It doesn't have to share your information because that's not necessary. Meanwhile, through the use of fine print, it has obscured the price of what it is selling as well as the product. This allows the website to potentially get more money from people interested in dieting than it would with a truly free sample or a straightforward selling proposition revealing the true cost. If you were a patient at the Mayo Clinic, the clinic would be prohibited from sharing your personal information with others. But on the diet site, you're not a patient. There's nothing stopping the website from using essentially all of its information in future solicitations or commercial dealings with you, including dealings on behalf of third parties. And there's nothing stopping the website itself from using your information in any way for its own purposes.

The website that the Mayo Clinic licenses is not alone in using fine print to cover its tracks. It's a standard business practice these days. Whatever you do, wherever you go, whatever you buy, consumers are confronted with an enormous volume of legal terms and conditions. No reasonable person reads it all, and in fact, it's probably not even possible to do so.

Look carefully at loyalty programs, for instance, which are rich sources of fine print. They are easy to join and good at collecting data. But the hoped-for benefits can be harder to obtain. Often the advertised benefits of these programs are not well defined. CVS Pharmacy's ExtraCare rewards program, for instance, advertises "coupons for instant savings," but there are exclusions:

Some restrictions apply. ExtraCare card must be presented to get these savings. Savings applied to total purchase with specified product. Excludes prescriptions, alcohol, gift cards, lottery, money orders, postage stamps, pre-paid cards and tobacco products. No cash back. Tax charged on pre-coupon price where required.

As for your CVS ExtraBucks rewards, in which you're promised to get 2 percent back from your everyday purchases:

Excludes alcohol, gift cards, lottery, money orders, prescriptions, postage stamps, pre-paid cards, tobacco products or items reimbursed by a governmental program. Customers must shop during the 45 day distribution period to receive their 2% and prescription ExtraBucks Rewards, which will be rounded down to the nearest $0.50. Members who do not spend $25 in qualifying purchases or who do not otherwise reach a minimum of $0.50 in ExtraBucks Rewards by the end of an earning period will not receive rewards and will not have earnings carried over.

But it goes on to exclude certain states and government programs and the like. Good luck figuring out whether you really are entitled to benefits. The arrangement seems transparently designed to suggest that you will get special treatment while in fact delivering as little as possible. In business terms, companies try to maximize the perception of benefits and minimize the actual cost.

Fine print is another useful tool for extracting the consumer surplus. All that legal language obscures both the price and what the customer actually gets, the product itself. Its purpose is to benefit the seller, and the seller has a key advantage. If you sell one product—take soap, for example—to lots of customers, it makes sense to hire a lawyer to write a contract that gives you lots of advantages. If, on the other hand, you buy hundreds of products from hundreds of sellers, it makes no sense at all to wade through all those legal terms. Consumers are asked to sign "contracts" written by sellers that the consumers don't even read, much less understand and consciously agree to. Consumers only learn what's in the fine print when it's too late. It comes up when they complain or ask for something they thought they should have gotten, and the seller says no, pointing out a provision in the customer agreement.

But the proliferation of fine print is significant in another way too. It's a catchall for taking advantage of customers. If you think companies won't use the growing knowledge they have about you to extract higher prices, think again. In many small and big ways, companies already take advantage of your trust. With more sophisticated data extraction and analysis, exploitation will only get easier, cheaper, and more pervasive.

Checking on Checking

Look at all the ways companies are already exploiting trust through the proliferation of fine print. Take something many people think they're pretty familiar with, the basic checking account. Today, there are about 100 million checking accounts in the United States. Without a checking account, it's difficult and often costly to do many simple transactions. In the past, checking accounts were fairly standard, simple products. Today they are a maze of complexity with rules and fees varying widely. So widely, in fact, that the typical annual cost of a basic account can range from zero to more than $700, according to a 2014 survey of checking-account costs by WalletHub, a consumer-finance information and social-networking website. "For such a ubiquitous financial product, one would expect consistency in disclosures and fee standardization," WalletHub wrote in a research report. "Unfortunately, the opposite is true. Consumers face disclosure practices and fee arrangements that resemble the Wild West."

Making simple products more complex is just one way that companies can extract more of the consumer surplus. Complexity hides the true price and nature of a product or service. WalletHub found thirty different types of fees associated with checking accounts. That's not a good scenario for customers who want to understand what the real price is and comparison shop. "The sheer number of different fees associated with checking accounts prevents effective product comparison and decreases the likelihood that consumers will find the best checking accounts for their needs," WalletHub wrote in its report on the transparency of checking accounts. To even attempt a comparison, WalletHub created five different consumer profiles in order to measure the different costs across twenty-five major consumer banks in the United States. For one profile, the "cash-strapped consumer," WalletHub found that the annual cost of a checking account varied from as low as $2.83 for Capital One 360 Checking to as high as $735.00 for M&T Free Checking (note the "Free Checking"!). WalletHub defined *cash-strapped* as a customer who overdraws twelve times a year, uses an out-of-network ATM once a month, and averages an end-of-the-month balance of $50. The big difference between the two accounts was the fee charged on overdrafts. Instead of charging a fixed dollar amount in overdraft fees, which is typical in the industry, Capital One charges an 11.25 percent annual percentage rate on the amount a customer overcharges. Another difference is that Capital One didn't charge fees on out-of-network ATMs. The fact that it takes an analyst to compare the cost of checking accounts is revealing in itself. How does an ordinary consumer have a hope of figuring it out? Wasn't more information supposed to be better for us as consumers? But it's not turning out that way.

With checking accounts, the general rule is: The less money held in a checking account, the more the account holder pays in bank fees. The biggest fees fall on consumers who occasionally overdraw their accounts, a surprisingly common practice among less well-off customers. The average annual cost of a checking account for a customer who overdraws an account once a month was $499.02. At the other end of the spectrum, according to WalletHub, the average annual cost for customers whose monthly balance never drops below $5,000 and who only use their own bank's ATM machines was $17.85. All those fees add up to big money for the banks. A 2013 analysis found that the banking industry made almost $32 billion in annual revenue from overdraft fees and some $8 billion in ATM-withdrawal fees. In a July 2014 study, the Consumer Financial Protection Bureau found that overdraft fees and fees associated with insufficient funds constitute the majority of all checking-account fees that consumers incur. It also found that transactions associated with overdraft fees are often quite small; in the case of debit-card transactions, the typical overdrawn amount is around twenty-four dollars and paid back to the bank in less than a month. Given that typical overdraft fees exceed thirty dollars, banks turn an unseemly profit on customers who have trouble making ends meet.

And fees on checking accounts have risen. A September 2014 Bankrate survey of ATM and overdraft fees found both at record highs. The average fee for using an out-of-network ATM rose 5 percent over the past year and increased 23 percent over the past five years. It now stands at $4.35 per transaction. The average overdraft fee set a new record high for the sixteenth consecutive year at $32.74. Free checking is fading away, with only 38 percent of noninterest checking accounts completely free of maintenance fees, down from 76 percent five years ago.

The first thing to notice about the checking account example is that the prevalence of overdraft fees means that some consumers have no idea how much the product will cost until they use it. Even with Capital One's much more reasonable fee structure, you can't tell what the ultimate cost will be unless you know in advance how much you will overdraw and for how long. It's part of a penalty pricing strategy that has been swept into many consumer businesses. Think about your cell phone. You typically pay for a certain amount of minutes per month, but if you go over, you expect a penalty. The same goes for driving. If you lease a car instead of buying it, you pay a penalty if your miles go over the limit at the end of the lease. Penalties for talking too much, driving too much, or spending too much are commonplace today. And that means that in many ways, consumers really don't know the price of what they choose to use until it's too late.

Another point to notice is that all those fees and charges associated with a checking account can change at any time. Banks can change their account agreement as they wish at whatever time they decide. They have to disclose fee changes, of course, but they can do that by sending a letter that looks just like a lot of other junk mail. At the moment, Capital One seems to offer the best deal. Customers might flock to open a Capital One checking account because there is no charge for out-of-network ATM withdrawals. But after a while Capital One could change its mind and start charging the same fees as everybody else, or even higher.

A final point to notice is that finance in particular is not bashful about getting vulnerable customers to pay exorbitant fees. There's some truth to the proposition that the less money you have, the more banks charge for their services. If you don't really need a loan, banks bend over backward to make credit available. But the more customers need their mortgage or credit-card loan, the higher the rate of interest charged. Of course, banks never put it in those terms. They talk about why people with reduced means are riskier borrowers than the wealthy. They have a point, of course, but the perverse effect of segmenting the market by levels of wealth is that banks wind up charging the highest prices to people on the tightest budgets. The approach can be counterproductive when it happens on a large scale. In the midst of the financial crisis, when banks suspected that Lehman Brothers was in trouble, they required Lehman to pay higher fees in order to conduct business, worsening the problem. The same thing probably happened to many American consumers as banks tightened credit and thereby precipitated defaults, which in a vicious cycle led to still more credit tightening.

Banks know a lot about their customers' finances. They use that knowledge to determine how much to charge for everything from a basic checking account to a mortgage. When they know your intimate details, they can and do make you pay.

The Flying Game

The inescapable fact is that travel from point A to point B is a quintessential commodity. Despite this fact, or more accurately because of it, airlines have ceaselessly sought out ways of segmenting the market to make more money. Prices change frequently, and new levels of service such as "economy plus" and "beyond first" are introduced. And then, of course, there's the matter of all the fine print tied to airline tickets and loyalty programs.

Most fliers recognize that airlines offer different classes of service. But few understand just how many different types of tickets there are. United Airlines, for example, uses thirty-eight different kinds of tickets, ranging from the top-of-the-line unrestricted first class to the lowly discounted economy fare. To get an idea of just how complicated the system is, consider this. United gives its best customers, the ones who buy unrestricted first-class tickets, a different deal depending on whether their flights are on planes with three classes of service or just two. If the planes have three classes of service, the passengers get more frequent-flier miles and slightly higher priority in United's pecking order.

From different fare rules to the newest additional fees to complicated frequent-flier programs, airlines have developed the ultimate cover for charging prices that reflect not cost but customers' willingness to pay. Take change fees, for example. For an arbitrary round trip from New York to Los Angeles, a discounted coach seat on Delta Airlines is offered at $378. The catch (actually only one of the catches) is that if you need to make a change, you pay a change fee of $200 plus the difference in ticket price, if any. On the other hand, you could buy an unrestricted ticket. Same plane, same seat, but no change fee. That option is offered for a mere $2,800. You'd be better off buying seven discount round trips and using the one that best matches your timing!

For the customer, the problem with the change fee is that no one can be sure whether he or she will want to, or have to, change his or her flight plans. The airline has stacked the deck in its own favor. Bring in the customers with the lowest price offer and then hit the unlucky, vulnerable few with a heavy fee.

Why can't passengers resell tickets through the airline or even on eBay? There's absolutely no reason other than to create a "gotcha" for the unlucky people who can't use their "discount" tickets. The purpose of transfer restrictions is to allow airlines to charge more when customers find themselves needing to change plans. It's a grab at the consumer surplus, plain and simple. If tickets could be freely resold, fare differences would immediately flatten and pricing would become more transparent. As it stands, transfer restrictions have the harsh side effect of costing a few unlucky travelers substantial penalties and causing others to carry on with trips they otherwise would not make.

Everyone knows airline pricing is based on supply and demand. Fares are more expensive during peak travel seasons, such as summertime, and to prime destinations, such as European capitals. So if a flight to Rome costs more than a flight to Milan, you'd think the demand for Rome must be higher or the supply must be lower. What's puzzling, though, is that you can pay a high price to a given destination but a dramatically lower price for the exact same flight if you agree to follow on to another destination.

The following is the result of an actual search for Delta flights to Rome in 2014. The round-trip, economy flight directly to Rome, leaving John F. Kennedy International Airport (JFK) at 10:05 p.m., costs $1,655. Now compare that to a round-trip, economy flight to Rome leaving JFK at the same time, on the exact same airplane, but with a connecting flight onward to Milan. The cost: $903. Delta will take a passenger to Rome for $750 less, provided that the passenger promises to take another flight, at the airline's additional cost, onward to Milan. If the Rome passenger didn't mind spending the time, he or she would be better off buying the Milan ticket and then buying another ticket and flying back from Milan to Rome because that would cost far less than $750.

Of course, in a free market, customers would simply buy the Milan ticket, stop off in Rome, and then discard the connecting tickets to Milan. Even better, they would sell the Rome-to-Milan connection to someone who wanted it. But airlines, clever devils that they are, make their own rules. The fine print says that if the passenger gets off in Rome and doesn't fly on to Milan, Delta cancels the rest of the ticket. It's all set out in black and white in fine print in the airline's ticket policies.

Airlines manage their profitability by segmenting the market for air travel and charging customers different prices for the same product. In this case, the market is segmented based on the demand for direct flights. Airlines know most people prefer the shortest route to their destination, so they make customers pay up for the privilege of flying direct. Perversely, it can make business sense for airlines to offer lower fares on indirect routes even though that wastes both the airline's and the customer's time and money if a direct route is available. It's just another way to encourage customers to pay more.

When prices become so obviously illogical, it's time to revisit the fine print and ask why airline tickets can't be transferred or resold just like most other property. Airlines want you to believe your security is at stake, but that's a canard. And while a small cost may be involved in making a name change, a dollar or two would easily cover it. After all, anyone can walk up and buy an airline ticket until shortly before takeoff, so why would transferring a ticket be any different? It could all be done very efficiently on the airline website. The Transportation Security Administration itself says there's not a security issue. The Secure Flight system that screens airline passengers can handle checks instantly, according to the agency.

Airlines strictly enforce the nontransferability of tickets so they can charge higher prices. If you can't use your ticket, airlines can keep the money you paid and sell another seat on the plane. They can also charge higher prices for last-minute travel and segment the market into ways that favor them. And they can charge lucrative change fees. In 2008, when JetBlue doubled its change fee to $100, it said it expected to earn about $50 million in additional revenue that year, largely from the fee change. Delta rakes in over $700 million a year from change fees.

There's no basis for the ticket-transfer restriction other than to allow airlines to extract surplus from customers. It's a bit of low-hanging fruit awaiting attention from the Federal Trade Commission, which could achieve an easy win by prohibiting airlines from maintaining such unfair policies. The restriction on ticket transfer may not even be legal in the first place due to existing legal doctrines prohibiting unreasonable restraints on assignment or alienation of property.

At least so far, airline-type restrictions on transfer don't show up throughout the rest of the consumer economy. Imagine a movie theater linking tickets to individual names and charging change fees before allowing someone else to use the ticket. Or imagine a grocery store that offers to sell a container of orange juice for five dollars and then offers the same container plus some milk for four dollars. That wouldn't happen, because customers could throw the milk away, give it to a friend, or sell it on eBay. Unlike airline tickets, orange juice and milk are still sold without further restrictions.

But there's no guarantee things won't change. One of the advantages of the Internet is that it permits sellers to almost instantaneously establish detailed policies for virtually any transaction and then change them at will. Customers are just one click away from agreeing to pages and pages of legal terms that can and will be used against them if the opportunity arises. So far, U.S. consumer protection regulators have been asleep at the switch, and courts seem reluctant to prohibit the enforcement of such one-sided arrangements. It's actually surprising that one-sided user agreements haven't already started creeping into the brick-and-mortar world.

In fact, they have. The rapid growth of loyalty programs, with all their terms and conditions, provides an easy path to get consumers to agree to terms written by sellers. To imagine where this is headed, look again at the airline frequent-flier programs. They are intentionally complicated, making them difficult to compare. And they change. In early 2014 major airlines like Delta and United changed their programs to reward spending rather than mileage. That solves a problem of the airline's own making because a long flight doesn't necessarily mean a more expensive flight. A short flight, in fact, can be far more expensive than a long one. For New Yorkers it's often less expensive to fly to Los Angeles than to Pittsburgh. And when longer flights cost more, the prices can be disproportionate. For instance, a flight westbound from New York to Los Angeles covers some 2,472 miles. Going east from New York to London is about 3,450 miles, almost 40 percent longer, so it's reasonable to expect a flight to London to cost more than to Los Angeles. What's puzzling is that a no-frills trip to London sometimes costs three to four times as much as a trip to Los Angeles. Airlines trying to reward lucrative customers recognized they needed to change, so the more you spend, the more credit you get.

But now we have a highly complex system for frequent fliers. For instance, look at Qantas. It changed its frequent-flier program to compete with other major airlines. That resulted in "a bewildering array of 120 defined accrual levels," reported IdeaWorks, a U.S. consulting firm. "The challenge faced by customers is the daunting complexity of the new method introduced by Qantas." Under its new system, Qantas has fifteen travel regions that combine with eight different fare categories to produce a matrix of possible frequent-flier points earned by a customer. That comes on top of a system that was complicated to begin with. Who even knows when they can redeem points and when they can't? Customers can either fly Qantas and hope for the best or give up and take their business elsewhere. The one thing they can't do is make a fully informed choice because airlines now use tiered point-redemption categories that make it far more complex to redeem points. And keep in mind that frequent-flier programs can change at any time.

Restrictions on transfer are just one way businesses tie up customers and charge them more. Other techniques include introductory discounts, automatically renewing contracts, automatic transfers from credit-card and bank accounts, penalties, cancellation fees, surcharges, multiyear contracts, and onerous user agreements. The cellular-telephone industry uses all of these tactics and more. It's all set forth in the fine print. Two-year contracts are the norm, requiring consumers to select expensive bundles of equipment, service, and insurance. Penalties and fees apply for exceeding data limits, and international service can be shockingly expensive.

Take a look at that user agreement with your cell-phone carrier and you will quickly see that it has all the rights and you don't. Look at a user agreement with Verizon Wireless: "You cannot assign this agreement or any of your rights or duties under it without our permission. However, we may assign this agreement or any debt you owe us without notifying you."

That's typical of the pages and pages in a Verizon Wireless customer agreement. Verizon can change the terms and the conditions and the prices it charges you at any moment, but you cannot change carriers without paying a penalty. Verizon holds all the cards in the event of a dispute because its terms require customers to accept arbitration and seemingly give up any right to participate in a class-action suit. That's a critical concession that many companies require customers to agree to these days. In practical terms, it means that the customer can never sue the company. If a company like Verizon Wireless rips off 1 million people for $100 each, no individual can do much about it. It's not worth pursuing in arbitration, or in court. But if customers could join in a class-action suit, they could take Verizon to court. Despite all the inefficiencies of the class-action tort system, real benefits do come out of it. The threat of class action actually does help keep companies in line. But if customers agree to arbitrate, they give up their rights to sue. An agreement to arbitrate sounds reasonable, but it's highly favorable to the company.

Tiered pricing is another common fine-print trick in cell-phone service in the United States. Providers say, "Tell us how many minutes or how much data you want to buy, and if you go over we will penalize you." Cautious consumers end up buying more capacity than they actually use, in effect paying more for each minute or gigabyte than the advertised price.

All the fine-print tricks in cell-phone user agreements add up to a substantial difference in the cost of cell-phone service in the United States compared with other countries. A comparison of two similar plans, one in the United States and one in Great Britain, reveals a marked difference. The monthly cost for typical smartphone service from a major carrier in the United States was pegged at $109.47 while a similar service in the United Kingdom cost $68.12.

Both plans include the same model of iPhone with sixteen gigabytes of memory. Both require a two-year commitment and allow unlimited voice minutes and unlimited texting. The plan offered by Three UK provides unlimited data and requires no up-front payment. With Great Britain's 20 percent VAT included, the plan costs forty-one British pounds a month, or $68.12 at the exchange rate at the time. The plan provided by Verizon Wireless required an up-front payment of $99.99 and then costs $90.00 a month, not including taxes. After spreading the up-front cost over twenty-four months and adding 17 percent tax, typical for the United States, the total comes to $109.47 monthly. But while the UK plan includes unlimited data, the U.S. plan does not. It includes two gigabytes a month with another free gigabyte during an introductory period. To put that in perspective, two gigabytes of data allow about fifteen minutes of music streaming a day and about ten minutes of video watching a day. If you run over, you'll see it on your bill.

The difference in pricing between the United States and the United Kingdom is not an anomaly. Ofcom, the regulator of communications in the United Kingdom, annually compares the cost of services provided to the British with other major nations, including the United States. It has found that for some years now, U.S. cell-phone services cost much more than those of European nations without any evidence of lower quality. Part of the difference in pricing has to do with the fact that UK consumer regulators require clear pricing information. In the United States, pricing tends to be confusing and comparisons between competitors are hard to make. Each product and service has different terms, conditions, and payment options. UK regulators also try to ensure that consumers are free to switch if they get a better deal while U.S. customers can be locked into multiyear contracts.

Throughout the economy, consumers are asked to sign on to "user agreements," standard forms that companies apply to anyone who purchases their products or services. In the past, these have tended to be standard, one-size-fits-all policies. But supported by big data, the technology exists for companies to slice and dice their user agreements, even to the point of offering each consumer a custom-tailored agreement and then changing that agreement in real time. It seems likely that user agreements will get a lot more onerous and become an increasingly effective way for companies to segment markets.

The Privacy Policy

No discussion of the fine print would be complete without a mention of privacy policies. "Your privacy matters to us," or words of similar import, are a common catchphrase. It's worth looking into the fine print of a privacy policy to see what it says. Take Google's privacy policy, for instance, which some observers consider the industry's best in terms of its user-friendliness and well-developed thinking.

The first thing you notice about Google's privacy policy is that it doesn't actually tell you very much. Essentially, Google can collect whatever it wants from users who sign up for any type of Google account. But then it can also collect whatever it wants from everybody else or whatever it learns from other sources. That includes everything from photos and documents to videos, e-mail, and browsing history. And Google uses cookies that it plants on your computer—intrusions and modifications no different from hacking—to track you wherever you go and during whatever you do on the Internet, regardless of whether you are using a Google product or not. The policy, when you boil it down, says Google collects what it pleases while users allow the company to hack their systems. Everything you click on or type or even say or look at; everything about your computer or mobile device and phone number; everything about your present location and home address; and even your future destinations, desires, and aspirations. It's all Google-bait, and a growing portion of all that data is winding up in Google's electronic filing system.

Google's policy says: "We may collect and store information (including personal information) locally on your device using mechanisms such as browser web storage and application data caches." According to the company, Google can use a computer or mobile device that you own—your property—for whatever it wants without paying you any fee. Browser web storage means the company can track you across all sessions, even after you stop using the browser, close it, and reopen it. The application data cache lets Google collect data even when there's no Internet connection.

Google makes a point of saying it will share aggregated, nonpersonally identifiable information publicly and with partners such as advertisers, publishers, and connected sites. There are two glaring problems with this. For starters, any data these days can be personally identifiable given sufficient context. A rapidly improving science takes seemingly anonymous data and "de-anonymizes" it, tying items back to particular individuals. Second, when Google says it only shares your data with advertisers, that's not much of a limitation. The company has a lot of advertisers, probably the majority of businesses. Third, Google doesn't actually have to give or share the information with a third party to achieve any aim it wishes. The company can actually use the information it collects on a third party's behalf without letting the third party see it. So under Google's policy, whatever any third party wants to pay for, be it good or evil, Google can do in exactly the manner most beneficial to that third party and to Google. Google doesn't need to give advertisers a list of the names of the vulnerable elderly who are lonely, a little confused, and easily duped. It can just send targeted offers from other companies to each of those valuable prospects. Acting as a middleman, the company has the best of both worlds. It can charge a hefty fee, and it isn't, at least not directly, responsible for any dirty work.

In fact, that's already what Google does with its targeted ads. It doesn't hand advertisers information about all the people interested in tennis balls. It tells customers give us your ads, tell us about your business objectives, and then we'll show those ads to the most relevant people. Google doesn't have to hand over your information for it to be used against you. The company can do that all by itself. Privacy is a big issue, but the concern is not whether Google shares information. The real concern is exactly what does the company collect, and how does Google use that data? The privacy policy is so broad that it's essentially meaningless. Google carefully avoids placing *any* meaningful limits on its opportunities to make money. Meanwhile, the privacy policy and Google's corporate utterances are carefully crafted to sound trustworthy. "Don't be evil," right?

The tone of Google's privacy policy is as concerning as its lack of substance. The policy authorizes data collection, surveillance, and hacking but implies these activities benefit users. That may be the case, at least in part. But it's clear that Google also does what it does to benefit its advertisers and other customers, and it would be absurd to think that Google doesn't look after itself first and foremost. Google has placed itself at the center of commerce, matching buyers and sellers via the most effective communication and advertising system ever devised. That role necessarily requires balancing the interests of Google users searching for information and sending e-mails with the interests of advertisers seeking sales and profits. It's an enviable position to be in—and a powerful one.

Google says it uses the data it collects to improve its products and "to protect Google." But the company won't reveal exactly what it does with consumer data or where it draws the line between the interests of users and the interests of advertisers. The corporate motto may exhort employees not to be evil, but the fine print doesn't say anything about what happens if somebody somewhere at Google *is* evil. With many thousands of employees, it's a little hard to believe that none are unscrupulous. But if an individual finds himself or herself on the losing end of some evil behavior, under Google's policies he or she can't do a single thing about it. The company makes no promises. When Google says, "We will not reduce your rights under this Privacy Policy without your explicit consent," it's a gratuitous and meaningless statement. It's meaningless because you don't have any meaningful rights under the privacy policy in the first place. So Google's statement is merely a way to make users trust the company.

Throughout the economy, fine print hides a host of abusive practices. Companies use it to set the terms of commerce, stacking the deck against their customers. Nothing is off-limits to those seeking profits. A series of *New York Times* reports reveals the ways consumers seeking health care are exploited and made to pay higher prices than they should. In one case, a patient undergoing surgery for herniated discs in his neck received a surprise bill for $117,000 from an assistant surgeon called in midway through the surgery. The assistant was out of network, so the patient's insurance didn't cover the fee. It's hard to imagine a more vulnerable consumer than an anesthetized patient in the middle of an actual surgery. What a selling opportunity! The articles pointed out that some doctors commonly practice calling out-of-network associates in during the middle of surgery, when the patient can hardly object, and the associates then bill for many times higher than normal rates. Those associates can do the same in return, calling the doctors in as assistants on their next surgeries or even, as appears to happen in some cases, splitting the exorbitant fees. Every doctor involved took the Hippocratic oath to "do no harm," a policy with a far more impressive pedigree than Google's corporate motto. But when money's involved, it's amazing how people justify what they do.

There are many other concerning cases. A September 2014 study by the Center for Public Policy Priorities found that up to half of all Texas hospitals that participated with United Healthcare, Humana, and Blue Cross Blue Shield had no in-network emergency-room doctors of their own. So even if Texas residents had the presence of mind to choose an in-network hospital during a medical crisis, unbeknownst to them, their bills would be substantially higher because the insurers don't cover out-of-network providers. The insurers don't fight it because they save money.

It's no coincidence that the most valuable lists of data for sale on the Internet today are lists of vulnerable people, particularly people with financial problems. When people face financial stress, they will do anything and pay anything they can to get out of it. The same holds true with regard to physical or mental infirmities. When sellers find out you are vulnerable—whether that means you have to fly on a certain date, or you are in danger of losing your house, or you need immediate help of some kind—they can charge accordingly.

Many people aren't concerned about the fate of people who can't pay their debts, because they assume that people with financial problems deserve what they get. The fate of people in financial distress should be a concern, though, because research shows that the majority of that distress comes from three sources: illness, job loss, and divorce. Not all of us will face those situations, but no one is immune.

The balance of power in consumer markets has shifted dramatically to favor companies. As consumers, the public is being segmented into smaller and smaller groups until at the extreme, each individual faces one-to-one propositions, a market of one matched against a far more knowledgeable and sophisticated seller. Around the world, companies compete to carve up markets and gather the spoils. Airlines buy up slots at airports. Mobile and Internet providers drive competitors to merge. Hospitals consolidate into regional monopolies. Using big data, the benefits of holding a monopoly, or even a bit of market power, have never been greater. And consumers have never been under greater threat.

The proliferation of fine print allows companies to price discriminate and customize user and privacy agreements. It allows companies to create tailor-made products and services that are nontransferable and therefore advantageous to the seller in the marketplace—but not necessarily the buyer. The proliferation of fine print hides the means sellers use to gobble up more and more of the consumer surplus, sometimes overtly and sometimes by stealth and subterfuge.

PART III

What Comes Next

7

The New Gold Rush

When gold was discovered at Sutter's Mill in the winter of 1848, San Francisco was tiny—fewer than eight hundred people living on the shore of a beautiful natural harbor. Within three years California was a U.S. state, and San Francisco housed 25,000 residents while hundreds of thousands passed through the Golden Gate. From 1848 to the present, the total amount of gold extracted from the "Golden State" would fetch more than $100 billion in today's money.

But there's another bigger gold rush happening today. Rather than California, it's centered in suburban Ashburn, Virginia. Instead of gleaming-yellow nuggets, today's prospectors stake their claim to subatomic particles stored in vast arrays of computer memory. The particles themselves have no intrinsic value, but the intricate arrangements in which they are stored constitute the most valuable physical asset ever created: big data.

Big data doesn't look anything like a gold mine. A visitor to Ashburn might be excused for failing to appreciate how important that town is to the global economy. Thirty miles from Washington, DC, Ashburn is a fifteen-minute drive north of Dulles International Airport. To the general public, the only clue that something important happens in Ashburn is the prevalence of large, warehouse-like buildings with little visible activity. Boxy and nondescript, on closer inspection these structures display some unusual features. For one thing, they seem to have a lot of cooling equipment. And for another, they exhibit industrial-sized electrical connections and row upon row of backup generators.

Ashburn's boring buildings house the Internet. Collectively, the servers they contain represent one of the greatest collections of computing power and data in the world. Although consumers are accustomed to thinking of the Internet as something "virtual," conjured to our screens as if by magic, in fact, every bit of the Internet is physical. Millions of miles of wires, cables, and fiber connect millions of computer chips and electronic components. Every piece, down to the last Phillips-head screw—even down to the last quark or electron—is real. And every last bit is *owned*, either by a person or an organization. As wonderful as the Internet seems to consumers, it is and always has been a business. While consumers blithely click and tweet and share, a few huge companies desperately struggle to gain control of as much of the Internet as possible. These companies are the data giants. And they come to Ashburn to connect.

Ashburn happens to be where one of the early Internet companies, UUNET, set up its operations back in 1987. UUNET later merged with the telecom giant MCI, which set up its own headquarters in Ashburn. Ashburn's growing communications infrastructure attracted America Online (AOL), which opened its headquarters there in 1996. As MCI and other companies added fiber to support the rapidly growing Internet, more computing giants followed AOL to Ashburn. Building paused momentarily following the "dotcom" crash in 2000, but after a brief interlude, the surviving titans of the Internet were building again in Ashburn. MCI itself was bought lock, stock, and barrel by Verizon in 2006. Today something like 70 percent of all Internet traffic flows through Ashburn and the surrounding communities, routed through one of more than forty large data centers.

One of the companies that came to Ashburn was Amazon. Best known as the "everything store," Amazon quietly established another business that sells computing power to all comers. Amazon Web Services, known as AWS, is the leading provider of computing infrastructure to independent businesses and organizations. AWS computers power not just Amazon but Netflix, Pinterest, Expedia, Reddit, and a long list of other websites and companies. AWS' enormous scale allows Amazon to charge low rates for only as much processing power as customers need, providing the ability to rapidly grow or shrink as desired.

Like others in the industry, AWS makes almost a fetish of secrecy. The company won't provide details on the size and location of its facilities or a precise tally of its amassed computing resources. Knowledgeable AWS employees are sworn to secrecy. It's become something of a parlor game for technology sleuths to estimate what AWS and other web companies have built. Little by little, a few facts have been established.

It's estimated that around 70 percent of AWS' entire capacity is located in or near Ashburn, in multiple facilities. One building known to be associated with AWS is 200,000 square feet in size. That's over four acres, about the size of Walmart's biggest stores, and typical for the data industry. Inside are racks upon racks of servers arranged in neat rows. The capacity for collecting and processing data is immense, and the electricity required could power thousands of homes. But that four-acre building is just a single facility. AWS operates dozens of data centers spread around the world, from Sao Paolo to Stockholm to Singapore to Sydney, serving companies such as the Brazilian airline GOL, the British consumer giant Unilever, and the Taiwanese social network Pixnet—and it adds more capacity every day.

The businesses supported by AWS require a lot of computing power. The movie-streaming website Netflix alone is thought to supply around one-third of the entire Internet's traffic. AWS isn't just running Netflix, though. While AWS servers deliver content, AWS and the businesses it serves vacuum up data and use it for reference and analysis.

When you order a movie from Netflix, the AWS servers are, in effect, privately making another movie, one in which you are the subject and the star. It's not for Amazon's entertainment. The unsleeping servers of AWS see more than you realize, and they never forget. Vast electronic brains in Ashburn and around the world study you very carefully and respond with ever-increasing intelligence. The service to consumers is remarkable and greatly valued. But the aptly named "servers" serve their owners in ways that many customers simply don't understand.

Like Sutter's Mill in Northern California, Ashburn may someday be memorialized as a kind of ground zero for today's great gold rush. For decades, companies and investors have descended on Ashburn in full cry, building their capacity to capture as much of the Internet as possible. Data centers popped up, followed by more data centers. Today every business depends to some degree on data. Collecting, analyzing, and storing data is how a company gets to know its customers and matches price and product to market demands. Even small companies can put together a few elements plucked from the mosaic of data, setting out who you are, your needs, your wants, your desires, and your resources. But only a handful of companies possess the data and the smarts to put together definitive pictures of millions of individuals. These are the companies that will call the shots. Although most businesses and consumers focus on day-to-day concerns, they remain largely unaware of the titanic struggle among the lords of data to accumulate data and facilities in order to own critical portions of the Internet. The ultimate goal of this handful of companies is not just to dominate the data industry but the entire economy.

World War D

Among all companies collecting and using data for commercial purposes, ten are poised to dominate. The names are familiar: Amazon, Apple, AT&T, Comcast, Facebook, Google, IBM, Microsoft, Oracle, and Verizon. They belong to a very exclusive club of the world's richest companies. Each of the "Ten" on its own is worth at least $100 billion. Together, these data giants are worth $2.6 trillion. No other ten U.S. companies can match that total.

The Ten have deep financial resources, and they tend to be highly profitable. Together, their profits exceed $270 billion a year, with another quarter trillion of cash on hand. Each of these firms owns key pieces of the Internet and is heavily investing to own more. They each started with a special advantage: Google knows what you want. Facebook knows what you pay attention to. Amazon knows what you buy and what you pay. Verizon and AT&T know where you are and what you transmit and receive. Comcast knows where you go online. Oracle, Microsoft, and IBM make the systems that make big data useful. Each of the Ten recognizes the importance of filling in the whole picture. It's no accident that Google has developed social media sites like Google+, Groups, Orkut, Blogger, and Hangouts. Or that Verizon and AT&T have developed super cookies, nondeletable tags that track the Internet activity of their cell-phone users. Microsoft offers a search engine, and IBM runs data centers. Each company has the financial means to compete on all fronts. The eventual winners of this worldwide data war, "World War D," will gain an immense prize: unprecedented economic power over huge portions of the global economy.

Like nation-states, the Ten form and break alliances while furiously spending in the digital arms race. They pay to build large data centers and the fiber and wireless networks that connect people and machines in every corner of the world. They also spend on developing new technologies. Six of the Ten rank among the world's leading research and development (R&D) investors. Some names could tell a story on their own: first IBM, then Microsoft, and now Apple.

These three companies each represented the pinnacle of success and corporate prestige in its era. In the 1970s IBM was the undisputed leader in computing hardware. In the 1990s Microsoft established itself as the leader as attention shifted to software. And now Apple is preeminent. That hardly means that IBM and Microsoft are finished, though. Even the seemingly least successful of the Ten still has the money, the infrastructure, the connections, and the brains to go back on the offensive and challenge the others.

While leadership in data itself has shifted, all of the former number-one players are still around and remain competitive. AT&T was the big dog in the 1950s and 1960s, followed by IBM in the 1970s, and then Microsoft in the 1990s. But each still exists with a huge business and can still compete with Google, Facebook, and Apple.

The Ten invest huge amounts in technologies both physical and intellectual. The amounts these companies spend on the combination of research and development and expanding capacity are impressive—collectively over $100 billion a year.

Even more impressive is the fact that these powerful companies orchestrate whole sectors of the economy. The telecom, wireless, and cable companies spend a relative pittance on direct R&D because they don't have to spend more. Their privileged position as owners of essential networks lets them buy the innovations of others. Samsung, for example, is the world's largest R&D investor. Samsung may build a great phone, but it can't turn it on in the United States without the help of a wireless company. So Samsung does the heavy lifting and then U.S. wireless operators resell those phones to nearly captive customers at a rich markup. Nice work if you can get it.

Amazon, Google, and Facebook have the edge in content. Everybody wants what they provide. But their business is at risk if a new

Company	Market capitalization	Cash	Annual cash flow (EBITDA)	Annual R&D	Annual capital investment
Amazon	144	7	4	7	3
Apple	647	25	60	5	7
AT&T	174	2	46	2	21
Comcast	149	5	23	—	7
Facebook	218	14	6	1	1
Google	357	60	20	7	7
IBM	159	10	25	6	4
Microsoft	383	89	33	10	6
Oracle	199	52	17	5	1
VZ	194	8	50	—	17
Total	2624	272	284	43	74

Source: U.S. Securities and Exchange Commission filings as of September 30, 2014, and closing share prices as of December 31, 2014.
Note: All figures in billions of U.S. dollars.

venture comes along and builds a better virtual mousetrap. So the data giants frequently buy up-and-coming companies and invest in others. They also hire a lot of people, offering comfortable jobs to the best and brightest. Google, for example, now employs more than 50,000 people. Those employees aren't corporate drones typing in the answers to our search queries. A decent fraction are technical geniuses trained in the world's top academic programs. With a little luck, Google's talented geeks will invent the next Internet phenomenon. And even if they don't, when an invention occurs elsewhere, Google can quickly copy it. As long as Google keeps those employees on board, they won't be working for, or become, a competitor.

The data rush is happening now. The Ten are furiously building capacity and adding services, hoping to end up with the right mix of software, users, and infrastructure that will make them indispensable, irreplaceable, and dominant.

The Data Industry

The value of data-driven lists has been growing ever since the invention of the mail-order catalog—which was a while ago, at least since 1498, when Aldo Manuzio first distributed a catalog of his popular book editions to whet the appetites of Venetian customers. With the growth of an efficient worldwide postal service in the nineteenth century (the original Internet!), mail-order companies grew into large firms. It became increasingly important to mail out catalogs to potential customers and avoid the expense of sending materials to people who wouldn't be interested. Companies kept records of who their customers were and used various means to identify the most promising new prospects. Before long, data brokers popped up: companies organized to help assemble mailing lists combed from directories and statistical records. Over the years these data brokers learned their trade, supplying names and addresses that are divided into categories for marketing purposes. Drawing from their accumulated experience and adopting technological innovations, data brokers created large databases of consumer information. Today, between 3,000 and 4,000 data-broker firms operate in the United States alone, and they sell a lot of data.

Data brokers collect a surprising amount of information about each of us. Along with our names, addresses, and phone numbers, data brokers know a lot about what we earn or borrow, how much we spend, and what we buy. They know if we pay our bills on time, and they have a pretty good picture of what we spend our time doing.

Like the global postal network of over a century ago, the Internet has transformed catalog selling. And it has also transformed the data-broker industry. Now data brokers offer a tremendous amount of personal data on virtually every person in the developed world. They scour the growing body of information available online and add it to their databases. So if you want the address and phone number of everybody within twelve miles of the Washington Monument who has two kids, speaks Portuguese, and drives a ten-year-old car, just ask. You'll have to pay for it, but you can get a pretty accurate list.

As laid out in a 2014 Federal Trade Commission (FTC) report, the core business of data brokers is to sell lists. Some lists aren't particularly intrusive. People appearing on lists of "Dog Owners," "Winter Activity Enthusiasts," or "Mail Order Responders" might not mind. Lists that focus on ethnicity and income such as "Urban Scramblers" and "Mobile Mixers" might be more sensitive because according to the FTC report, both groups include a high concentration of Latinos and African Americans with low incomes. Other lists highlight age, such as "Rural Everlasting," which includes single men and single women over the age of sixty-six with "low educational attainment and low net worth" and "Married Sophisticates," which includes thirty-something couples in the "upper-middle class . . . with no children." More sensitive still are lists focused on health-related topics or conditions, such as "Expectant Parent," "Diabetes Interest," and "Cholesterol Focus."

All of these lists, and more, may be had for a price. It's easy to imagine perfectly legitimate uses of the information. It's just as easy to see that in the wrong hands, personal information can be used against consumers. Among the more valuable lists available for sale are lists of people behind on their mortgages. The threat of losing one's home powerfully motivates one to borrow, even on unfavorable terms. It's not difficult to imagine less than scrupulous finance companies luring in customers with products that seem beneficial at first but ultimately prove very costly. One need look no further than payday lending for a good example.

The extent of information in the hands of data brokers is impressive. According to a government report, a single data-broker firm maintains a database with 3,000 data elements for nearly every person in the United States. That means lists can be overlaid to produce a very detailed picture of individuals. Showing up on a list is one thing. But showing up as "Dog Owner," "Diabetes Interest," "Urban Scramble," and "Direct Mail Responder" starts to paint a picture.

If it makes you uncomfortable to know that thousands of data brokers sift through your data wake and then sell a detailed picture of you, you probably aren't alone. You might be more concerned to learn that the data-broker industry is almost entirely unregulated except for narrow categories of credit and health data, which are off-limits. But even those seemingly protected areas are vulnerable to disclosure by inference. For example, your doctor can't tell the data broker Acxiom about your health status. But what you buy; your web surfing and e-mail traffic; and what you disclose on forms, surveys, and questionnaires is all fair game. Data brokers are more than willing to create a list of people who are probably diabetic, even if that's not confirmed by their personal doctors.

What's even more concerning, though, is that data brokers are a dying industry. Their core business depended on the economics of the direct-mail and telephone-solicitation businesses. A company like Acxiom can tie its database to your name, phone number, and maybe your e-mail. That's not trivial, but it pales in comparison to what the data giants can do. A company like Google or Facebook or Verizon doesn't need a data broker because it already receives a far richer data stream than what the data brokers can access. If you use Facebook, you provide a mountain of intimate data to Facebook. The people you know, the products and services that matter to you, and your activities and your interests are all revealed. What's more, the data giants can see your life unfold in real time on a granular basis and can begin to predict what you want and where you are going.

The amount of information collected by data giants, and the potential usefulness of that information, dwarfs the data-broker industry. The data giants can study our e-mails and phone calls, track our web surfing and mobile-phone use, tally up our buying and selling, and follow where we are at all times. Google doesn't need a list of "Dog Owners" with millions of names on the list. Google has a list of one—you—that doesn't care whether you own a dog but that knows you click on pet food ads, as well as myriad other things about you. And Google has other "lists of one" for hundreds of millions of other consumers. The advent of granular, comprehensive, real-time data exceeds anything the data brokers are capable of.

The Economics of Data

The world of data has its own economics. If you know one thing about one person, you don't have much. If you know one thing about nearly everyone or nearly everything about one person, you have a little. But if you know nearly everything about nearly everyone, you've got something priceless. Essentially, data giants are middlemen who connect buyers with sellers for a fee. Google, for example, takes a place among the premier content providers in the world. Every day, the company handles millions of searches for its users. But mainly, it creates lots and lots of lists. Google became what it is because its lists are very useful to millions of users. But in nearly every case, what a user wants is not provided by Google itself. Google just connects what the user wants with a list of relevant web pages. Google's famous web crawlers search the Internet, making lists and rendering those lists to users.

All companies face growing competition online, where a local business is no nearer than a competitor on the other side of the world: just one click away. When ordinary companies add more computing power, it's a necessary expense, something required to make and sell their offerings. But for the data giants, each new data center is an end in itself and a competitive weapon. Traditional companies accumulate information about a narrow range of activity. Companies record who their customers are, where they are located, what and how much they buy, and the prices they pay. In the past, companies ascertained rudimentary facts about their customers by observing, by asking questions, and by using data brokers. But they lacked the data, the access, and the analytical resources to assemble a granular picture of customers.

The data giants are fundamentally different. Companies like Amazon or Facebook know (or infer) not just who you are but what you are like. They know not only where you are but they can guess where you are going. They don't just know what you are doing right now—they have a pretty good idea why you are doing it. And they make excellent guesses about what you will do next, guesses that grow more accurate every day as you go about the business of daily life while being carefully observed by the data giants.

For the data giants, the Internet isn't an abstraction, and it certainly isn't a utopian space where all are treated fairly. The Internet is a loose collection of physical equipment owned by competing groups. It's a commercial battleground where a few companies dominate the field. The most important bits of the Internet are in the buildings like Amazon's facility in Ashburn that look like big-box stores.

What consumers don't realize is this: *They* are in those structures. The most detailed report prepared by analysts working for the Stasi or the KGB (or our very own CIA for that matter!) doesn't begin to compare with the comprehensive data wake shed by each consumer. Every minute of the day we shed data in profusion. Every movement, gesture, word, and keystroke creates additional data. Computers, tablets, cell phones, and sensors all around us pick up huge and ever-growing quantities of intimate information, then record, tabulate, and analyze it. For the privileged few with the access and ability to read it, a data wake shows what happened, why it happened, and increasingly what will happen next.

Today's data giants vie for what is likely to be the richest commercial prize in history. The history of technology is full of great enterprises. More than a century ago, the Industrial Revolution spawned giant enterprises: companies like Standard Oil, U.S. Steel, and American Tobacco, which dominated whole industries. The giant trusts delivered unprecedented profits and built individual fortunes never before possible. The Ten are positioning themselves to dominate not merely a single industry but many industries at once, perhaps even entire economies.

That's because data giants are positioned to act as middlemen on virtually every transaction, matching buyers with sellers while getting paid for that role. Gradually, the data giants are already capturing a growing share of the economy's surplus. Knowing the customer intimately allows them to set various prices quickly and accurately, tailoring prices to individual need and the ability to pay from moment to moment. The more you need an item and the fewer your options, the more you pay. Engineering each transaction applies not only to pricing. Given sufficient data, quality and service can be individually tailored as well. A data giant can ascertain the minimum quality and service each customer will accept. Capturing a growing portion of the consumer surplus by charging more for almost *everything* represents an enormous commercial prize, a fortune bigger than has ever previously been possible.

The Producer Surplus

The massive collection of data doesn't only affect the consumer surplus. Companies also risk losing their profit margins, the mirror image of the consumer surplus. Virtually all businesses sell their offerings for some degree of profit. The amount of profit on each sale varies depending on many factors. Just as in the case of consumers willing to pay something more for their purchases if they had to, companies

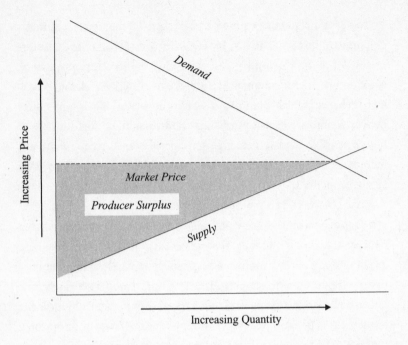

would be willing to take a lower price if they had to. Whenever a company makes a sale, there is necessarily an acceptable lower price that still delivers a profit until the point of indifference, when the company doesn't care whether a given sale occurs. Added up across the entire economy, the total profit made by sellers represents the producer surplus.

Like the consumer surplus, the aggregate producer surplus is a very large quantity. Corporate profits as a whole add up to something in the neighborhood of $2 trillion a year, and profits to the owners of unincorporated businesses add more than $1 trillion more. Businesses don't give up their profits without a fight, but the data giants have already started nibbling away at this more than $3 trillion prize.

Individual companies tend to be very reluctant to reveal how much they make on each sale, referred to as their "margin." It's an accepted principle of business that a buyer who knows the seller's margin can demand a better price, squeezing the margin and cutting into profits. In theory, if the buyer with sufficient clout knows the details, he or she can take all, or nearly all, of a seller's margin.

In the past, figuring out a seller's margin wasn't easy. Sellers guard their margins as trade secrets. But as with consumers, big data is gradually changing the balance of power for sellers. Given sufficient information, an astute buyer can deduce the seller's margin despite the seller's efforts to conceal it. Walmart, to take one example, has made a science of studying its supply chain and squeezing supplier margins at every opportunity. Walmart's extensive knowledge of not only its current suppliers but all other alternatives in the marketplace has allowed the company to bargain from a powerful position. The suppliers can't pretend they are offering their best prices when Walmart knows full well they are still making money. Walmart scientifically studies its suppliers' profits and very accurately judges about how much it has to pay. And given Walmart's giant scale, few sellers can just refuse to do business with it.

But even Walmart isn't a true data giant. While it has an impressive capability and scale, the company lacks a truly massive data funnel that would allow the pervasive collection of data in real time across the economy. The data giants are positioned to study companies as well as individuals, and the data wake left by companies is a rich trove. Historically, companies have protected themselves by operating their own data pools and requiring confidentiality agreements with workers. Over time, those protections will erode as the ability to maintain the secrecy of individual facts becomes a thing of the past. Secret formulas and manufacturing processes can be photographed with cellphone cameras, stored on miniature memory devices, and transmitted instantly around the world or published for all to see. Eventually, individual secrets will all but cease to exist, and the business paradigm will shift from creating value out of particular information to creating value from very large bodies of information. As data giants continue to vacuum up granular information in real time, they create an asset so vast that it can't be stolen or copied. Not because it's protected, but because it's so big.

Look at wages, for example. For a data giant, identifying all of the workers at a given company would be child's play. Location data from phones, cameras, and road sensors readily reveal who comes to the office. E-mail, web, phone, and travel records fill out the rest of the picture. Other sources fill out the details: roughly how much is earned and who is hired or fired, all in real time. The data giants can effectively study a company's workforce and fairly easily draw conclusions about a company's costs structure.

Intellectual property is another area with falling barriers. Historically, companies have gone to great lengths to protect their secret formulas and methods. But the falling cost of collecting and storing data leads to increasing opportunities for secrecy breaches. Imagine a manufacturing plant with a proprietary manufacturing process. Even if the intent is entirely innocent, over time, a set of pictures taken inside the plant will collect on Facebook and other photo-sharing sites. Employee birthday photos, bulletin-board pictures, and other seemingly innocuous items contain background clues that can be teased out via big data. With all the attention and patience of an archaeologist, but operating at lightspeed, the vast electronic brains of a data giant could, in theory, assemble a mosaic revealing the machinery and layout inside a manufacturing plant. With all their resources and capabilities, substantial companies are considerably less vulnerable than consumers to the predations of a data giant. But eventually, the massive collection of data will overwhelm all efforts at secrecy, putting even the largest companies at risk.

Individual secrets—a formula, a process, a price—will readily be discerned through the collection and analysis of data. In the end, the only remaining secrets will be the huge troves of data in the hands of the data giants, assets too massive to copy or exchange. No one but a data giant will control the resources to understand and use the treasures that lie within.

The data giants have begun down a path that leads to almost godlike omniscience. There is now a foreseeable prospect of knowing what every individual will pay for every single thing at each moment in time, as well as knowing what every seller or manufacturer will charge. The difference between the most an individual will pay and the least a seller will accept, the "surplus" of the entire economy, is the potential reward. With sufficient data and analytic power, a data giant is well positioned to charge for matching a supplier to a consumer. At the maximum, the data giant can absorb much or all of the entire surplus so that the consumer pays all he or she can pay, and the producer ends up with the least it will accept.

The Third Surplus: Labor

Along with the consumer surplus and the producer surplus, labor represents a third target for big data. Like any other sellers, workers sell their skills and efforts. The labor marketplace has historically been among the most inefficient areas of the economy, with large costs falling on companies seeking to identify and hire employees. Workers also face their own difficulties in identifying appropriate opportunities and negotiating pay. These widespread inefficiencies give rise to excess unemployment, labor unions, and myriad delays and costs that together constitute a significant drag on the labor market.

Big data has begun to fundamentally change the relationship between workers and employers. With the massive collection of granular employee data, companies can increasingly micromanage the output and productivity of each individual. Eventually, the crude science behind time-and-motion studies will be refined to more scientifically measure achievements in the workplace.

Workers are in a potentially precarious position. The tremendous information imbalance between the employer and the worker makes it difficult for an individual to figure out the value of his or her contribution. What's more, companies tend to be secretive about what they pay each worker. Individuals have limited means of assessing the "market" rates for their jobs.

Companies already harness the power of data to increase their bargaining power with workers. Electronic workplace surveillance, e-mail and phone records, and web-surfing histories provide a trove of data useful not only for weeding out bad apples but also for influencing desired behavior and negotiating pay. Companies have more opportunities than ever before to assess who is looking for a new job and who is not, who might leave a job, and who will stay no matter what. And companies have a whole range of opportunities to modify behavior. Policies against drugs, alcohol, smoking, and overeating— even outside the workplace—can now be backed up with intrusive surveillance and data collection.

Take the case of a single mother in St. Louis employed as an office worker until fired for publishing an anonymous blog salaciously detailing her amorous escapades. Despite taking care to keep her work life separate from her private life and blog, she was unable to fully hide her identity online. Thanks to the total recall of Twitter's search engine Topsy, her supervisor discovered the connection between her real name and her provocative blog, leading to her dismissal. Whether or not one approves of racy blogging, her story is a cautionary tale about the perils big data holds for employees. Few legal protections exist for employees when employers disapprove of off-duty behavior, and whatever protections do exist tend to be narrowly interpreted.

As massive data shifts the power balance from workers to employers, it shifts even more power to the data giants. Your company may be able to detect if you have been in e-mail contact with a recruiter, but Microsoft or Google or Verizon knows whether you have an interview, and when. The data giants are well positioned to sell their services to companies seeking to manage their workforce. Taken to the extreme, a data giant could be able to define the terms of employment across large populations.

The Power of the Middleman

Amazon provides a good example of the enormous economic potential for data giants. Because of its scale and its accumulated knowledge of suppliers, the company is well positioned to bargain for cost efficiencies and lower margins from its suppliers. Amazon's ownership of important data infrastructure, the server farms of AWS, for example, gives the company a huge window on the economy through which it can obtain granular data from millions of sources.

If Amazon knows it can charge an individual a bit more for a product, the company doesn't have to share that extra money with a supplier. Amazon can just keep it. Today the company's profits are not very impressive compared to its sales. Retailing is competitive, and Amazon has not, at least so far, figured out the magic formula to make big profits while driving competitors out of business. But the pressure Amazon places on competitors is intense, and the future profit potential is tantalizing. That's a plausible explanation of why Amazon's stock trades at a high value despite its meager profits. If Amazon gains the upper hand in retailing, profits will follow in due course.

Amazon's rapid rise to the top tier of retailing has given the company substantial market power. In book publishing, for example, something in the neighborhood of one-third of the market belongs to Amazon. So when the company reached an impasse with the large publisher Hachette, it simply stopped selling some of the titles published by Hachette imprints. Determined purchasers still found the books from other sellers, but the cost—and message—to Hachette was clear.

Amazon's retail network and big-data capabilities are easy to understand. It's a little less obvious how Facebook and Google are becoming powerful middlemen on billions of transactions. After all, Google and Facebook aren't retailers. But they are advertisers. When you click through an ad from a data giant and make a purchase, the data giant gets its cut. How much Google or Facebook gets is not apparent to the customer because that happens behind the scenes. But it would not be difficult for any of the data giants to negotiate as follows: When the consumer clicks on an ad for toothpaste, the data giant knows who he or she is. The field is currently in its infancy, but before long the data giant will be able to assess what the consumer is willing to pay. In a microsecond or two following that first click, Facebook can convey a message to the toothpaste seller: "I have a customer interested in your product who will pay $5.00 for it." Because Facebook can capture very detailed knowledge of the seller's cost structure, in the next millisecond Facebook reveals the catch: "The Facebook commission will be $2.50 for this customer. Would you like to accept this proposal?"

The building blocks of market dominance are already in place. In his book *The Search*, John Battelle tells the story of an online shoe retailer, 2bigfeet.com, which sells large sizes of men's shoes. Early in the company's history, the website's popularity naturally put 2bigfeet .com near the top of Google searches for oversized shoes. In 2004, without warning or explanation, Google changed its search algorithm. As a consequence, 2bigfeet.com all but disappeared from the Internet, demoted from the first page to the fiftieth page. After the company's business nearly dried up, it didn't take long for 2bigfeet.com to figure out a solution. The shoe seller began buying ads from Google and shot right back to the top of the results, where it remains today.

The 2bigfeet.com story is a neat illustration of how powerful Google's business model is. The company's original search technology gained popularity and users. User growth increased Google's scale, providing the company lots of data to improve its search technology. Over time, Google outpaced all of its competitors in search, and now the company's immense scale makes it almost impossible for most companies to avoid. Like it or not, if a business wants to be found online, Google is well positioned to charge a toll. Nobody is forced to pay, of course. Any business that is comfortable with not appearing as a search result can completely ignore Google. But there aren't many companies left that can afford to be invisible to online search. Meanwhile, the data giants are creating a new class system in the economy. At the top are organizations, like Google or Facebook, that have the data and machines to orchestrate vast portions of the economy, gobbling up surplus and extracting value on a scale never before imagined. Below them are lesser companies and businesses that carve out specific niches, perhaps holding a patent or (for now) a secret edge that can't be readily duplicated. And at the bottom will be a huge number of businesses and consumers increasingly disadvantaged by their complete inabilities to contend with the data giants on equal terms.

8

The End of the Free Market

Imagine going to a restaurant a few years hence. A place you are familiar with. You didn't make a reservation, but it was almost as if they knew you were coming. They greeted you by name and seated you right away at your preferred table. The waiter offered up a special dish just for you. And of course you bought the bottled water, perhaps one too many drinks, and your favorite dessert. It was all a little expensive—the place always seems a little expensive—but they did a great job. On the way home, you wondered whether you really needed that glass of the dessert wine and the special appetizer. But there's no doubt that you thoroughly enjoyed the meal.

The restaurant seemed to know what you like because they did, in fact, know you very well. While you were on your way to the restaurant, an alert with your name and picture popped up on the screen in the host's podium. Cameras took in your face, height, posture, body type, and hair and eye color and compared all of that to your last visit, confirming your identification.

Although you didn't make a reservation, your cell phone gave away your location and put a name and an e-mail to your face. The data service told the restaurant early on that you were likely to arrive. Then as you approached, geolocation from your phone alerted the host. By the time you stepped inside, the host could greet you by name with complete confidence. The menu and pricing were triangulated from the restaurant's stock of ingredients and your personal data.

As cameras recorded nonverbal clues, other sensors picked up your voice and comments at each stage of the meal, whether good or bad, as well as other items not limited to just the restaurant or the food. Your chair recorded your weight before and after and noted your shifting position along the way. The exact duration of each meal element was recorded and managed.

The menu wasn't printed on paper. You selected your meal from a lightweight tablet computer screen. Because you are a repeat customer, the menu choices (and the prices) were just for you. The first drink was discounted just enough so that you couldn't resist it. When it came to the second, what the hell, you only live once. In collaboration with the data giant that provides back-office services to the restaurant, a detailed psychograph of your desires and propensities allowed the restaurant to almost perfectly anticipate what you would buy and how much you would pay.

Lots of other data backed up the psychograph. The restaurant glassware spoke volumes. What, how much, and how fast you drank was just the tip of the iceberg. Back at the dishwashing station, the plongeur ran a quick swab around the rim of your glass and tossed the tip into an analyzer. From a tiny drop of saliva, a minute amount of unique DNA was retrieved and fully sequenced. Your trip to the bathroom produced a trove of data. Although the restaurant would be quick to assure you that no human reviews the sounds and images of your bathroom performance, the machines never sleep. Your sound and motion was thoroughly digitized, analyzed, and recorded. "Intelligent" plumbing performed further tests. The restaurant now has a more complete medical record of you than your physician ever had.

Perhaps you didn't notice, but on the back of the menu was the following printed blurb:

OUR PRIVACY POLICY: In collaboration with our data partner "Giant," we collect personal data that we may use to provide, maintain, and improve our services and to develop new ones. We will not share personally identifiable information without your consent. Our privacy policy may change, but we will not reduce your rights without your consent.

It's doubtful that you read it, but even if you did, you probably would have felt okay about the vaguely comforting words. The restaurant and its data partner are certainly okay with it. It's easy for them to promise not to reduce your rights because under that policy, as a practical matter, your rights are approximately nil.

Working with its data partner, the restaurant gave you exactly what you wanted and collected some extra revenue for that. The restaurateur does a steady business, nothing to complain about. He can't seem to get ahead, though. That's because every time receipts go up, lo and behold, the data partner increases its charges by a similar amount. Over the course of a year, there's a lot of money going out the door to the data partner. But there's no way the restaurant can compete without data. Lots of other restaurants are willing to give a great experience based on big data.

The Data Squeeze

The "restaurant of the future" doesn't exist. It's hard to imagine that anyone is taking DNA from restaurant glasses today, and restroom surveillance seems beyond the pale. Although companies are, in fact, working hard to develop psychographic profiles of consumers on a mass scale, most of this work is at a crude stage. Restaurants are not varying their menus to reflect insights from big data. At least not yet.

But the technologies and analytics described in the restaurant story actually do exist, even if only in early versions. The forward march of technology is relentless. The price of sensors, computing power, connectivity, and data storage falls dramatically year after year. The capability of wringing actionable intelligence from mountains of data increases even more quickly. And the systems and business processes that allow product customization and fast pricing improve every day. Unless limited through grassroots consumer demand or top-down legal authority, all of the consequences described in the restaurant tale are virtually certain to occur, even if the exact methods differ.

And that will usher in a new economic order. Conceivably, a single data giant, or more likely a few data giants, will hold unprecedented power over what consumers know, what consumers are offered, and what consumers finally pay. With their granular, real-time knowledge of consumer surplus, data giants will tailor commerce to individual tastes and circumstances. Personalized customization and restrictions on transfer will erode the resale market, making arbitrage impossible. The mass market will disappear into an immensely complex, data-driven market in which prices vary from minute to minute and individual to individual. Standard goods and services will evolve into a multidimensional tapestry of customized offerings. Fortunes on a scale never before possible will be created. The age of the consumer sovereign and commoditized products will finally expire.

The imbalance of information will be profound. No person or entity lacking access to the data and the analytic resources of a data giant stands even a remote chance of bargaining effectively with a data giant. Take comparison-shopping sites, for example. For airline travel, web services such as Expedia or Kayak appear to offer a broad survey of airline offerings. And in fact, they did that reasonably well, at first. But airlines have been quick to respond. Some, such as Southwest Airlines, simply don't participate. You can't price a Southwest ticket on Kayak because Southwest won't let you. Others opened up a range of customized features that makes comparison difficult. So what if you book the lowest fare if you unexpectedly find yourself paying a fee that was not readily apparent on Kayak. And there's nothing to stop the comparison sites from favoring one product over another, at the consumer's expense. Even more importantly, a search on Kayak reveals data reflecting a single point in time. The airline pricing engine that you are unknowingly bargaining with has vastly more information. It knows what customers are buying and what they are rejecting as it shifts the price from moment to moment. You will never know if you can get a better price if you wait a day to book or if you should have booked earlier. No one has the time to sit on Kayak for days to watch prices, and even if they did, an individual lacks the analytic chops to discern how many seats remain open and the optimum time to buy. The pricing engine, on the other hand, contains very accurate information about inventory, demand, and competition and will always out-bargain the individual except in cases of pure random chance.

When you add up asymmetric information, price discrimination, mass customization, and restrictions on the transferability of products, you see nothing less than the systematic dismantling of the free market. What remains is a fatally flawed economy in which natural monopolies flourish and immense economic power is overwhelmingly concentrated in the hands of a few.

Granular Monopoly

Americans have always worried about monopoly power. The Boston Tea Party ended with the destruction of tea imported to Boston by the British East India Company, a monopoly established in 1600 under the reign of Queen Elizabeth I. In fact, concerns about monopolies have been around since antiquity. The word, used by Aristotle when fretting about a dealer who had cornered the market in olive presses, comes to us from the ancient Greek. Both hated and feared, in ancient times monopolies were somewhat benign by modern standards. Ancient technologies lacked sufficient advancement to enable monopolists to exploit their power fully. Limitations on communication, transport, and the powers of legal enforcement made monopolies harder to spread. And a far less specialized economy meant that most people could make do for themselves without having to pay a monopolist for a product or service.

In the medieval era, major European cities were characterized by guilds: business or trade associations that controlled a whole sector of the economy in an urban region. Bakers, weavers, goldsmiths, doctors, lawyers, and moneylenders, to name a few, banded together in each city to maintain prices and to exclude or discipline competitors. Although monopolistic in effect, guilds shared some of the characteristics of labor unions by protecting the wages and income of the members of each trade. Customers paid a premium, but the benefits of guild membership were distributed broadly among guild members in each city.

Advances in technology, particularly the transportation technologies that led to the discovery of the New World, set the stage for the first recognizable large-scale monopolies. Stock companies—organized to exploit lucrative trade opportunities linking distant trade partners with Europe—grew to immense scale, producing fortunes for their investors. Among the most successful was the London-based East India Company, which dominated trade between India and China and much of the rest of the world for two hundred years. The company obtained a legal monopoly granted by the British Parliament and then maintained that monopoly through a series of skillful political moves. The company's reach was truly global, its presence resented as much as respected. When Samuel Adams and the Sons of Liberty held the Boston Tea Party in 1773, the British East India Company's tea ended up floating in the harbor.

With the Industrial Revolution came a paradigm shift, the beginning of even more powerful monopolies. The population shift from the countryside to cities established masses of people without the possibility of making do for themselves. After all, apartment dwellers can't grow their own food no matter how much they may want to. The rapid economic expansion that followed industrialization offered many benefits, but it simultaneously increased the scale and value of business monopolies. Global industrial companies, sometimes owned and controlled by a single individual, could gain market power in extensive areas. The remarkable efficiencies of their immense scale allowed industrial monopolists to extend their reach while at the same time creating and collecting economic surplus.

For a leading example, look at the petroleum industry. After beginning in Russia in the 1820s, oil extraction spread to the United States in the 1850s. From the 1860s onward, the industrialist John D. Rockefeller embarked on a remarkable campaign to take over and consolidate the petroleum industry. He used brutal tactics, demanding that competitors sell to him or face ruin from predatory pricing. By 1888 Rockefeller had gained control of over 88 percent of the U.S. oil industry. Thanks in no small part to Rockefeller, public outcry at the growth of giant monopolies resulted in the passage of antitrust laws that required the breakup of Rockefeller's Standard Oil empire into thirty-three separate companies. Although a single person could no longer wield the power of Standard Oil, the immense Rockefeller fortune was hardly diminished. Much of the Standard Oil group was reassembled over time and is recognizable today as the giant Exxon-Mobil, still among the most valuable companies in America.

But ExxonMobil is not America's most valuable company anymore. Microsoft held that distinction for a time, but in late 2014 Apple's value exceeded the runners up, ExxonMobil and Microsoft, by more than $200 billion. It's not a coincidence that both Apple and Microsoft are data giants. In fact, data giants have the potential of becoming the most valuable companies imaginable. So long as antitrust remains lax and consumer protection is lacking, big data and advanced analytics will march onward toward fully exploiting the commercial power of data. Data giants have established a new paradigm for monopoly. Standard Oil developed an industrial monopoly by gaining the power to set prices on standardized products over broad geographies. Data giants are chasing *granular* monopoly, a phenomenon never before possible. The granular monopolist holds the power to dictate price and quality on an individual basis, in real time, over immense populations. That is, on an incredible scale. And granular monopoly threatens the very bedrock principle of today's economy, the "free market."

When John D. Rockefeller assembled Standard Oil, the company had a virtual stranglehold on oil, but it had no way of knowing customers in detail and no way of changing prices in real time. Esso, the familiar rendering of Standard Oil's acronym, set its prices by making educated guesses at what the market would bear. Prices were changed whenever advantageous, but with a pronounced time lag. It could take months and sometimes years for Standard Oil to detect that it should adjust a particular price for a given customer. Keeping track of prices required a large bureaucracy, slowing down the process. By skillfully exercising his industrial monopoly as best he could with the tools at hand, the Rockefeller *paterfamilias* made the largest fortune of his day. Yet as large as Standard Oil's profits became, the company left a lot of consumer surplus on the table. An industrial-age monopolist could nibble at the consumer surplus, but the process of setting monopoly prices in the mass-market era still left big chunks of consumer surplus in the hands of customers.

Granular monopolists, on the other hand, have new opportunities. A handful of granular monopolists won't have to guess at what consumers will pay because they will already *know*. Using that knowledge, a granular monopolist can set pricing for every single customer and change that pricing from moment to moment. It can deal with consumers one by one from a position of advantage, putting not just a portion but the *entire* consumer surplus at risk. This moment in time represents a turning point. We are living through a historic change in the world's economy, one as significant as the Industrial Revolution.

The End of the Free Market

In common parlance, "free market" means an economy in which buyers and sellers willingly exchange goods and services for mutual benefit. Economic theorists calling themselves "microeconomists" have gone so far as to mathematically "prove" that the free market leads to optimum results. Or so they claim, at least. In developing their seemingly elegant proof of the superiority of free markets, microeconomists make some interesting assumptions. Those assumptions amount to an idealized marketplace, not just a free market but a *perfect* market. So in order to gain the supposed benefits of a free market, various practical obstacles must be overcome. The more the real world deviates from a perfect market, the less optimum the overall outcome will be. At the extreme, a few players or even a single individual can benefit from an imperfect market while millions or even billions pay the price.

First, a perfect market depends on a large number of buyers and sellers. With many consumers willing and able to buy and many sellers willing and able to sell, prices will reach their natural equilibrium. Not everyone needs to actually participate in the market as long as everyone has the ability to get in on the action. When price fluctuates, people will become buyers or sellers as their circumstances dictate. In a perfect market there are lots of exchanges, but opportunities to make exceptional profits—selling high or buying low—simply vanish.

Second, a perfect market has no transaction costs. Whenever it costs something to buy or sell, an astute player can take advantage of that cost. Buying and selling houses is a good example in which transaction costs are significant. Because houses are unique and every buyer desires something different, it's not easy to match a buyer with a seller. The real-estate brokerage industry has sprung into the breach, offering to secure deals in return for a percentage of the price. Americans take it for granted that a 6 percent real-estate commission is roughly fair (the U.S. average is about 5.4 percent), but most don't know they are paying three times as much as homeowners in, say, Great Britain, where the average broker fee is less than 2 percent. Paying nearly 6 percent extra for every house means that everyone (except real-estate brokers) winds up with less house than they could otherwise afford. Some sales, in which a willing seller would accept a little less, will simply never happen. Families saving up for a home must work a little longer before buying.

Third, a perfect market depends on commodity products. If the widget Sam offers for $1.02 is exactly the same as the widget Sue is selling for $1.01, Sam is going to have to lower his price. Any time products or services vary within a given category, it destroys the perfection of the market. That's a big reason why the grocery store stocks so many obviously different products. Each seller tries to distinguish its product—it can be as trivial as a different fragrance—and loudly proclaims uniqueness, which makes head-to-head comparisons with other products or brands correspondingly more difficult. A customer unused to drinking Coke or Pepsi would hardly notice the difference between the two. But millions of consumers around the world pay extra to drink their personal choice.

Last, the perfect market runs on information. To reach the "free market" ideal, buyers and sellers must have all the relevant facts. If one side knows something important that the other side doesn't know, it can benefit at the expense of its trading partner. That situation plagues the used-car market. Owners know their car's history and are usually aware of its problems. Buyers are more or less in the dark and sometimes get a raw deal indeed. By some estimates, the entire market for used cars is depressed because of the information imbalance between buyers and sellers. But this could never happen in a perfect market.

It doesn't take much to realize that the real world is a long way from a perfect market. Consumers may choose from whom to buy, but in many cases those choices tend to be somewhat limited. Goods fall into categories, but categories have splintered into subcategories, and individual customization is increasing. Transaction costs are still quite significant, whether counted in hours searching the web or in miles driven from store to store. Perhaps most important of all are the large and growing information asymmetries between consumers and firms with access to data.

The technology-enabled breakdown of the free markets has already begun. For a good example, look at the closest approximation of a perfect market ever devised: the stock market. The stock market is an impressive creation. It trades in perfect commodities. Every share of, say, Microsoft is exactly the same as every other share. Stock trades are reported immediately. Long ago, stock dealers maintained written price sheets or wrote prices on chalkboards. Later the telegraph, then the ticker tape, allowed traders all over the country to follow the action. Now a Bloomberg terminal screen is *de rigeur* on Wall Street, where the prices of securities show up in fractions of a second.

Other features enhance the efficiency of the stock market. Detailed disclosure rules require companies and securities dealers to publish material information on a timely basis. An energetic financial press ranging from major publications such as the *Wall Street Journal* to newsletters, blogs, and analyst reports supplements the required company disclosures. Various rules, including insider-trading restrictions and short-swing profit prohibitions, are meant to dissuade persons with inside information from taking advantage of unknowing counterparties. At the federal level, the U.S. Securities and Exchange Commission employs some 3,500 people to enforce the securities laws, and each U.S. state has additional regulations and personnel. Overall, the stock market is about as close to a perfect market as has yet been invented.

But even with all of its advantages, including perfect commodities and a plethora of information, the seeming efficiency of the stock market is constantly under attack from market operators. Among the most important features of the stock market is the real-time report of trading, the so-called "ticker." It's easy to assume that the quoted price for a stock accurately reflects the latest trade between a willing buyer and a willing seller. But increasingly, stock trades are done privately, where the details are never made public. Technology makes it simple for large stock operators to trade shares off of the public exchanges in "dark pools," members-only stock exchanges in which only a select few can see what's really happening. When the New York Stock Exchange reports Verizon shares at forty-eight dollars, the dark-pool price could differ significantly—but the public would never know. In an industry in which information is as good as gold, private exchanges provide a secret edge to members—data the general public never sees.

Other market players rely on speed to capture opportunities. Algorithmic trading using massive computing power to gain an edge can happen in the blink of an eye. By strategically positioning data centers, electronic traders can set themselves up to act as middlemen on millions of transactions. When offers to buy or sell are transmitted around the country, a well-located electronic trader can pick up the signal microseconds earlier than anyone else and trade in advance. So when a buy order enters the system, the electronic trader quickly buys and then resells those shares into the original buy order for an instant profit.

Insofar as dark pools and electronic trading are profitable, and evidence suggests they are *very* profitable, those activities put a drag on the efficiency of the overall market. The biggest profits in finance, though, lie in inventing obscure new products available from only a few dealers, or sometimes a single source. When financial types extol the virtues of financial innovation, this is what they mean. You can practically see dollar signs flashing in their eyes. Derivatives—securities "derived" from other securities or commodities—can be customized for specific customers and are often unique. There's no market price to refer to, so customers must bargain with the dealer. Customers can neither see what others pay for comparable products nor the profit margin when the dealer slices and dices the risks and sells them off to other purchasers. In illiquid markets the customer is on his or her own while the dealer can see all the cards.

So although technology has created a vast amount of wealth and efficiency in the stock market, it can also be used to undermine markets and extract value. We take stock markets for granted, but in fact, no one knows whether we could be nearing a tipping point where the total amount of electronic trading, dark pools, and customized derivatives will overwhelm the general public's trust in the financial sector. It's interesting to reflect on the tremendous gains in the stock market over the years. No one would argue for turning back the clock to 1850 when Paul Reuter tied stock prices to carrier pigeons. Both the overall economy and the financial sector are immensely wealthier than they were back in Reuter's day. But it's interesting to note that the financial-services sector, as a share of the world economy, has grown rather than shrunk. Perhaps that's not a fair measure of the sector's overall contribution, but it should give pause to those evangelizing the benefits of new technology in economic transactions.

Technology can undermine other markets in comparable ways. The knowledge gap between big integrated companies and consumers has always been large. A traditional company like General Motors (GM), for example, knows a lot more about the cost and quality of its cars than any consumer will likely ever know. GM also knows a lot about pricing, carefully studying how many cars it sells at varying price levels. But old-school manufacturers like GM can only offer relatively crude versions of product customization: Think of the company's different models, option packages, and colors. And although car dealers size up potential retail customers, they often lack insight into basic questions, such as whether the prospect has been shopping at other dealerships.

The data giants conduct business on another plane. They can instantly offer products and services from any seller around the world to a buyer. Product customization isn't a problem. If the customer wants it, a data giant can find it for him or her or, if the product doesn't exist, arrange for someone to make it. Data giants don't have to guess whether a particular customer has been shopping around, because they know. Data giants employ a virtual real-time feed showing where the customer has been, what he or she looked for, and what prices he or she saw. The data giant has the means to assemble a detailed psychograph of each customer showing what the customer cares about and what the customer will likely overlook.

As data giants achieve increasing power in the economy, the free market faces threats from every side. Product customization, opaque pricing, and complex contracts are poised to expand from their natural origins in the world of services to all other sectors of the economy. Ultimately, even commodity markets will be broken down; the ability to differentiate and track a single ear of corn (perhaps even a single kernel!), when combined with rapid-fire trading and complex derivatives, will render market prices invisible to all but a few. Each consumer mass market will grow ripe for extinction, gradually leaving individual consumers to bargain on their own against the superhuman knowledge of the data giants. The transaction costs of avoiding data giants will increase as their reach extends throughout the economy, dictating winners and losers. Absent some broad-based resistance from the public, the collective information asymmetry will increase faster than any individual or ordinary group can keep up with.

Without a new paradigm, the public will never be able to watch the watchers. A data giant like Amazon can add servers, storage, and analytics faster than any organization that is not a data giant itself. Try as the news media, academia, and consumer watchdogs may, their reports will always come too late, as fast-moving prices and products render any consumer-oriented analysis stale even before it is published.

The "free" market is often conflated with one characterized by little government regulation, in which buyers and sellers are not constrained (as conservatives think) or protected (as liberals imagine) by legislation and rules. Currently, the market for data fits that description, being almost entirely unregulated. To the extent that regulations offer any privacy for individual health records or banking information, the protections are in fact quite limited. The gross amount of data available is very large and growing daily while the science of de-anonymization progresses in parallel. It's an axiom of computing that given sufficient context, *any* piece of data can be tied to a specific individual. Putting certain records off-limits is becoming increasingly ineffective.

The truth about the "free market" is that it is the specific, intentional creation of a broad coalition of consumers, business people, and governing elites acting with the benefit of millennia of hard-won human experience. Structure and governance are essential to the free market, and government is an essential, though often ignored, ingredient. Self-proclaimed free-market evangelists have sometimes decried environmental- or consumer-protection regulations while taking for granted the government's essential role in creating and securing money, prohibiting fraud, and enforcing contracts, each of which is essential to modern markets.

So far, the data giants have built businesses and stupendous fortunes by collecting and cleverly exploiting data from the rest of society—both businesses and consumers. Government regulation has been practically nonexistent. The data giants guard their own privacy jealously, refusing to reveal the extent of their data collection and the purposes it serves. Simple questions go unanswered as companies compete for mastery. Try to find out how much computing power Google deploys, and you will meet virtual silence. By virtue of their huge size, not to mention their one-sided user agreements and extensive government influence, the data giants regulate themselves when it comes to collecting and using data. The market is "free" only in the sense that the public, via the government, has been largely silent. But that's not to say it's free in the sense of increasing the freedom of society as a whole. The technology of big data and advanced analytics is the most advanced mechanism for mass influence ever devised. Left unchecked, big data spells the end of the free market as we have known it.

The macroeconomic effect of the end of the free market will be a general rise in price levels as the masters of data capture enormous profits. To the consumers, it will be something like living in an airport. They will have choices; nobody will hold a gun to their heads. But the choices will be based on what the data giants elect to offer, and the prices will be higher than what we are accustomed to. You know what it's like when you're at the airport. A bottle of water that normally would cost one dollar costs three dollars. A sandwich costs ten dollars. Consumers will be forced to pay elevated prices for most of what they buy because they are trapped in a filter bubble, one they might not even be able to perceive. And on an individual level, there will be other important effects. A person who really needs something—think of needing a kidney or a tank of gas in the middle of the desert—can in theory be forced to part with everything he or she has. So a general rise in price levels will be punctuated by occasionally extreme episodes of price gouging, when the data trap springs shut on a needful consumer. Although it's not widely known, it should come as no surprise that among the most valuable lists peddled by data brokers right now are those that reveal who is in financial trouble. From the point where companies know a customer's vulnerabilities and limited options, it's a very short step to the point of exploitation. The upshot of the end of the free market as we know it will be a large transfer of wealth from the general public to the most powerful companies in the economy. Although the mass market and the twentieth century created mass affluence, the ascendancy of data giants holds the prospect of less general prosperity—and even the potential for mass pauperization.

No one will be immune to the effects. In fact, in the commercial-data revolution, the wealthy have more to lose than anyone else. Mass markets, with standard products and transparent prices, provide economic benefits—consumer surplus—to virtually all members of our society. The amount of surplus, though, varies with a consumer's wealth. At a given price, a product delivers proportionately more surplus to a wealthy consumer than to an ordinary Joe, because the wealthier you are, the less a single dollar means to you. So as markets break down into individual transactions, the amount of surplus a data giant can grab from each consumer is greatest among the wealthiest. Think of it: If Bill Gates really wants a drink from the only restaurant in town that is still open, the price could be a lot different than for an ordinary working stiff who wants one just as bad.

When a seller knows a wealthy person intimately, it can easily charge a premium on everyday transactions. What multimillionaire is going to quibble about being overcharged by a few dollars for a Coke? After all, customers who spend time in five-star hotels might be excused for thinking it's fair to pay ten or twenty dollars for a canned drink. Back in 1992, when then-president George H. W. Bush was campaigning for reelection, he was accused of an amusing gaffe when a newspaper reported his amazement at a supermarket scanner, technology in use for more than fifteen years. Perhaps unfairly, the report saddled the president with the image of a wealthy patrician unused to doing his own shopping. But the supposed gaffe wouldn't have resonated if many ordinary people didn't have their own experiences with wealthy but out-of-touch compatriots. Clueless consumers, especially when wealthy, provide fertile ground for commercial exploitation via big data.

The accumulation of data threatens the very foundation of the American way: the free market. That's not to say that capitalism is threatened, nor that markets will cease to exist as they have for millennia. But the ability to understand *everyone* on a granular level, in real time, and simultaneously to control what each person is able to see, shifts the balance of power so dramatically that the *freedom* of markets is at risk.

But surely there are laws to protect us? After all, we live in a highly civilized society governed by centuries of accumulated knowledge and laws designed to protect the people.

The frightening truth is that no consumer protections or laws exist to prevent companies from extracting every last penny from us. Current laws against price gouging only apply in times of emergencies, for example, after Hurricane Katrina. Price discrimination laws apply to companies, not consumers. In most industries, no rules limit price discrimination at the consumer level, and there are certainly no laws against customization. When you add to that the fact that federal privacy laws have not been updated for e-mail, cell phones, or social networking, nor has the Electronic Communications Privacy Act of 1986, it becomes clear that consumers are on their own.

Monopoly laws provide little comfort. A fierce intellectual assault led by Robert Bork and others successfully undermined the philosophical basis for antitrust enforcement. Decades of lax enforcement and narrow judicial interpretations have deprived U.S. antitrust laws of much of their original potency.

Still, for the moment, individuals retain vestigial protections against the invasion of privacy. A few restrictions remain, limiting the analysis of snail-mail and voice communications as well as direct observation within the home. Some other data—medical records, banking details—retain at least some protection. But like the human appendix, these protections have become essentially irrelevant. The broad range of Internet, e-mail, and telephone data has been yielded up not only to government enterprises but also to commercial enterprises. Instant communications and 24/7 commerce beguile individuals into giving up immensely more control than they appreciate. The government has been fully complicit, with its own reasons for scooping up information both compelling, such as for disrupting violent plans, and disturbing, such as for managing electoral outcomes or promoting commercial interests.

The race is on to know us intimately. Companies want to extract as much data on customers as they can and set up data-information streams before the lid is blown off. When lawmakers finally put the pieces together and understand what has happened, it will be too late. The systems will be in place, and the companies will grow so powerful that not much can be done. While no one is monitoring them, Google, Facebook, Verizon, and the like are racing to the finish. America's technology and social-media giants have criticized the U.S. government for its data collection, only to remain silent about their own.

9

Data Environmentalism

The Environmental Awakening

A century ago, "environmentalism" as we know it today was a fringe idea. That's not to say that concern for the physical world did not exist. In the scientific community and the educated public rose a growing awareness of nature's complex organisms, systems, and interactions. But the *environment* as a subject hadn't yet crystallized. The great unowned backdrop that supports and enriches the pageant of human existence was not perceived as under threat. Air, water, minerals, organisms, the great unending currents and circulations of the atmosphere, the oceans, and the molten rock on which the earth's crust floats are all so vast they were almost unseen and taken for granted. Rendings in nature's fabric caused by urbanization and industrialization were lamented, and the passing of the old ways of life was mourned. But humanity lacked a basic understanding of the accelerating nature of environmental change and little considered the idea that humans could cause irreversible global damage. And the belief that all people share a similar interest in the well-being of "Mother Earth" seemed a rather remote concern.

Throughout the twentieth century, technology, development, and industrialization advanced in parallel. International trade touched record levels, creating the tightly integrated global economy we see today. Goods, services, and people moved continuously in intricate patterns around the world with increasing speed and efficiency. The telephone, and later the computer, hastened worldwide commerce. Meanwhile, political concerns leaped beyond traditional local bounds to engage the entire world, most vividly during the First and Second World Wars and only a little less so during the Cold War. Every corner of the earth was brought into the modern system.

Gradually, a tremendous change in perspective affected people around the world. From its beginnings in the nineteenth century, the environmental movement made massive gains in the second half of the twentieth century. By 1962, when Rachel Carson's *Silent Spring* burst upon the scene, an eager public sought answers to the problems of chemical pollution and rampant development. Carson vividly described the threats of pesticides and development, imagining a future without the gentle creatures we so fondly treasure; a "silent spring" in which once the sweet bird sang. Her book became a landmark, giving shape to the inchoate concerns of millions of readers. By inspiring a sense of the magnitude of what was at stake and offering a different path forward, *Silent Spring* created a new appreciation of humanity's impact on nature. Following the publication of Carson's book, the environmental movement gained widespread support and merged the efforts of creative thinkers, political activists, and government officials to bring about dramatic changes in the way our society relates to nature.

In a sense, the ideas in this book are, at a basic level, an extension of the environmental movement. Much like the physical oceans, ocean-sized quantities of data surround and support us. Like the natural environment, the virtual world of data has become so rich that we spend an increasing portion of our lives immersed in it. Whether in commerce or government or arts or entertainment, data is the fastest-growing part of our world.

And like the resources of the physical world, data has always been available. For millennia it was the occupation of scientists and scribes to measure and record discrete elements of the world's information. The pace of data creation has gradually accelerated over time. Almost five hundred years ago, Andreus Vesalius published the detailed structure of the human body. In the same year, 1543, Copernicus announced that the sun, rather than the earth, inhabited the center of our local space. Together, they touched off a scientific revolution, an expansion of data and information that has never ceased since. Around 1650 Europe entered the age of reason. Newton published his mathematical principles in 1687; Lavoisier identified oxygen in 1778. In 1896, as the modern age began, Henri Becquerel discovered radioactivity. Personnel at Bell Labs invented the semiconductor transistor in 1947, setting the stage for the eventual development of the Internet in the 1990s. Today the majority of the world's population has no recollection of life before the information age.

Each scientific era built on earlier discoveries, producing intellectual advances at an accelerating pace. What's different today, though, is that human capability is augmented by thinking machines. Their speed and computational power have created an entirely new phenomenon. Historically, thinkers have had to choose whether to look at a narrow area in fine detail or cover a broader territory without the same precision. Today scientists can have their cake and eat it too, undertaking the precise, granular study of extremely broad topics.

Like the environment, the world of data holds tremendous promise. We stand on the brink of knowledge previously undreamed of. The advances that can be derived from huge data sets hold great promise in mathematics, medicine, physics, and engineering.

Even greater advances are predicted in the social sciences, a field in which large amounts of accurate data can inform economics, politics, sociology, and business. Like scientific data, social data has been collected for millennia. Caesar Augustus ordered the census of the Roman world that set in motion the events recorded in the New Testament. Italian moneylenders invented modern accounting in the 1400s. The English physician John Snow carefully mapped a cholera outbreak in 1854 London, deducing the culprit to be polluted water. The Gallup public opinion polling firm got started in 1935, permanently changing elective politics.

Until a few decades ago, the principal advances in both the physical and the social sciences stemmed from manual labor. Whether due to a single researcher in a lab counting spots on a microscope slide or a thousand census takers going door to door with notepads, data was typically collected, recorded, and analyzed through painstaking human effort. The process of gathering data was laborious and slow, and researchers brilliantly chose what data to seek and collect. But overall, only an infinitesimal quantity of the world's available data was ever collected and recorded by hand.

Information technology fundamentally changed all fields of knowledge. Since the invention of the transistor in 1947, the cost of obtaining, recording, and analyzing data has steadily fallen according to Moore's law. Propounded by Gordon Moore in 1975, Moore's law posits that the capability of low-cost computer chips will double every two years. Since then the law has proven remarkably durable, resulting in major advances in the speed and accuracy of computing. Similar to the way the effects of industrialization started out small but ultimately profoundly changed the entire planet's ecosystem, the steady progress of electronics has led to immense impacts on the data environment. In the pre-electronic age, it was a sufficient objective for an ambitious scientist to know *something*. For the first time in human history, our most brilliant minds can plausibly approach a far more profound objective: to know *everything*.

It sounds far-fetched. Omniscience, after all, is the god-like property of myths, not a proper subject for human ambition. But the scope

and scale of data collection, combined with the speed and sophistica-
tion of analysis, has created a resource so rich that, even bounded by
current capabilities, it begins to approximate full knowledge of discrete subjects. Progress is relentless as year after year, the cost of data
and computing power falls.

The implications for our society are as profound as the impact of
human activity on the natural environment. Before the revolution
in human consciousness that we call environmentalism, it wasn't
thought possible that humans could alter the earth as a whole. Similarly, until the advent of the Internet, it was impossible for firms to
collect intimate, real-time information from entire populations. But
today, for better and for worse, the data environment rivals nature in
its importance and in its complexity.

That data leads to knowledge is manifest, and knowledge is power.
The question, then, is how the awesome power arising from big data
will be used. The stage is set for exploiting immense amounts of data
extracted from a panoptic array of sensors. There are important political concerns, to be sure. But the commercial and economic implications are both greater and more immediate. The struggle for
economic power is more likely to be the source than the result of political change. Our society's general prosperity, the hard-won balance between capital and labor, has begun to fray. The golden potential for knowledge from data shines temptingly, but it continues to be
tarnished by polluting, exploitative behavior. Personal data, particularly granular data recording the details of each individual path
through this brief mystery called life, is rightly the possession of each
individual. Large bodies of personal data must be treated as public assets held in trust for the general welfare, not private property ripe for
exploitation by a few at the cost of many.

Our fondest hope for this book is to inspire an environmental
movement for data. At its outset, what we think of now as the environmental movement existed only in the minds of a haphazard collection

of fringe thinkers. The general public's understanding of planetary resources and ecosystems was limited. The skies and oceans were conceived as boundless, free, and unaffected by human choices except in very localized ways. Long ago, if someone introduced a noxious substance into the air or the water, redress was only available if close neighbors could prove direct damage from the pollution. Anyone whose damage was latent, difficult to prove, or occurred far away was simply out of luck. The mental construct of limitless resources (excepting land, a divisible and ownable asset) served society fairly well for a time.

Rapid advances in chemistry and the growing scale of industrial enterprises began to cause a real and potential harm to the landscape, organisms, and people that was qualitatively different than in the preindustrial era. Species extinctions, mass illness, profound environmental degradation, and even worldwide climate change have since come to pass. Gradually, through the determined efforts of forward-looking people, the public has gained an understanding that emitting substances into the air or the water as much as one likes is problematic. Over time, the results of the environmental movement have been remarkable.

Today, whether you prefer fresh fish from the Chicago River or a starry night sky over the Thames, in many densely populated locations the environment is cleaner, more healthful, and more pleasing than it was a hundred years ago. But the process of raising environmental awareness to face newly perceived threats will always remain an ongoing challenge. Even after decades of careful research and journalistic reporting, a surprising fraction of the public is unconvinced that human activity has warmed our climate and threatens to change the earth's surface. So the environmental movement continues.

The environmentalism of data will require a similar, extended effort. Like air and water, data surrounds us. It's essential to our way of life, something our modern economy can scarcely do without. And like pollution, the environmental challenges posed by data are fundamentally a matter of scale. When a neighbor keeps pigs, the noxious smell of manure can seep across property lines to affect near neighbors. That was historically a small-scale problem, and legal remedies evolved over time. But what if your neighbor builds an industrial factory farm? Large-scale intensive hog farms house half-a-million pigs, producing immense quantities of waste. The smell emanating from waste lagoons can be considerable and affect a wide region. It's not simply a matter of one individual impinging on the rights of another. It's an issue in which an integrated commercial organization, for its own profit, impinges on the rights of a large population. An environmental issue.

The same principle holds true for data. It has always been possible for those with the means to hire a private investigator to collect personal data on anyone they wish. Following a subject, taking photographs, and sifting through garbage yields a lot of information. But that's painstaking work, far too expensive to be done for anything but very important reasons. And it can backfire if the investigator goes too far or if the subject catches on and takes steps in response.

Collecting and using data by hand can be important individually, but it is too expensive for most purposes. The vast majority of people will never have to contend with a traditional investigation into their private lives and can reasonably expect not to. But the small-data paradigm for investigations is long outdated. The number of data sources, which is already large, grows daily. The quantity and detail of collected information and the ability to collate, process, and store all that data grows exponentially. Meanwhile, ever-expanding networks and linkages of the global telecommunications system make it possible, for the first time, not just to collect huge bodies of data but to assemble, combine, and manipulate many of them at once. For the first time in history it has become plausible, at least in theory, for a single party to collect an approximation of all the data that exists, to update that collection in real time, and to study all that data with superhuman speed and thoroughness. The intricacies of the systems and software in use today exceed the understanding of all but a small coterie of scientists and network engineers. Perhaps one thousand people—out of 7 billion—thoroughly understand the global system in which the data giants operate.

Data presents a new environmental concern. It is now possible to collect, retain, and deeply understand not just some but *all* of a person's data. That possibility opens up prospects for harms and abuses entirely new to our society. From our DNA sequence to our online browsing history, personal data paints an intimate picture of who we are. It's no longer just part of the landscape, a boring and almost inaccessible statistical shadow cast as we go about our lives. For many practical purposes, data *is* our environment. Unintelligible to the unaided eye, the ones and zeros recorded in machine memory reveal the riveting, tragic, and sometimes salacious details of our lives.

And it all happens in real time, constantly updated and leaving a near-perfect record of the past. Growing rapidly, changing from minute to minute, the World Wide Web can finally lay claim to the accomplishment of an age-old dream: the creation of artificial intelligence. The scale and complexity of the Internet, fueled by the creative and scientific input of untold billions of users, surpass ordinary human understanding. Yet immense and powerful machines quickly navigate this intricate virtual realm, finding and returning answers to human queries and carrying out the hidden intentions of their owners with a speed that borders on the magical.

For a large part of the world's population, Google Search (or a similar search using a Google competitor) is the lens through which one navigates and assesses the world. If something doesn't show up on Google or a competing search engine or platform, then for all practical purposes, it can't be found. And if it can't be found, it might as well not exist. If a person can't be found on Facebook, or a product can't be bought on Amazon, then millions of users consign that person or that product to the void.

This new capability, the extension of human intelligence into a richly furnished virtual realm, transforms our perceptions of the world, of nature, and of each other. Humans interact with the external world in two ways: directly, through our five senses, and indirectly, through various media, including writings, sound recordings, telephones, and television. Beginning with Neolithic cave paintings and picture writing, media have steadily claimed an increasing share of our mental attention. If you start with cave painting and then chart the path of media technology from the first creation of coherent texts 4,500 years ago; through the invention of paper and printing 2,000 years ago; to the advent of movable type 1,000 years ago; to the penny press 200 years ago; to the arrival first of movies and radio, then TV, then broadband Internet, you see two clear trends. First, the quantity of data created has steadily increased over time. And second, the amount of time individuals spend interacting with data has increased as well, taking up a growing portion of our lives.

Digital Environmentalism

Around the world, environmental philosophy has permeated society. Limits on pollution, the preservation of undeveloped land, zoning restrictions, the protection of species, recycling, and energy efficiency are accepted elements of modern life. Today most nations recognize the profound environmental challenges that lie ahead: climate change, population growth, species loss, and habitat destruction.

That awareness would never have happened without a gradual learning process, whereby increasing numbers of people learned the scientific facts and adopted shared concerns. Through the bruising process of politics, increasing support for "green" policies grew into a consensus and finally was translated into law, affecting not only our current behavior but our innermost thoughts about future human progress.

In contrast, the ideas of data environmentalism are in their relative infancy. Twentieth-century writers like George Orwell laid out a framework for thinking about data in the context of a totalitarian government. But until now, privacy was not a commercial or economic concern. Only major governments were capable of mass surveillance, and only governments could benefit from the panoptic knowledge that remotely justified its cost. But that's no longer the case. The falling cost of acquiring and using data on a mass scale has opened up commercial possibilities far exceeding the scope of government to date. The threat from the commercial use of huge quantities of data is more immediate and, in important aspects, more extensive than the potential for government abuse. Commercial entities, by their very nature, act on behalf of their owners, unaccountable to the general public. Constitutional and legal protections against government intrusion into individual privacy don't apply to companies acting on their own behalfs.

Since Edward Snowden walked out of the National Security Administration (NSA) with 65,000 secret documents, it's no longer possible to ignore the tremendous reach of government data collection. But the most important details in the Snowden disclosures were the sources of much of the NSA data: commercial entities. The fact is, data giants possess, in some respects, more data than government agencies. Meanwhile, they operate with less oversight and fewer restrictions.

The environmental movement to protect personal data begins with education. The public must be informed about the amount of data collected and how exploitable that data has become. The next step is to consider the implications for companies, workers, and consumers and to appreciate where large-scale data collection is headed. Organization is essential. And patience. The natural environmental movement had its start long before the movement gained currency and clout. The Sierra Club dates back to 1892, and the National Audubon Society started in 1916. Generations passed before the Environmental Protection Agency (EPA) was established in 1970.

Incursions on the physical world, though, unfold at a slower pace than in the data environment. The rate of data creation is accelerating considerably faster than the global gross domestic product. If the data environmental movement takes one hundred years, vast changes in our society will be complete before a significant counterweight arises. That's not cause for despair, though. The same network that enables big-data players to collect information also supports a wide range of interpersonal communications, from texting to Twitter. Once sufficiently informed and motivated, individuals can organize and coordinate political activity faster and cheaper than ever before. There is at least the opportunity to take action in the near term.

Unlike the traditional environmental movement, data environmentalism is not conducive to pictorial representation. One can't underestimate the emotional appeal of the beautiful nature photography of Ansel Adams or Galen Rowell and its effect on environmental consciousness. In our image-saturated media, the abstractions of data environmentalism would greatly benefit from compelling visual expression. It's a difficult challenge and an immense opportunity for today's artists, filmmakers, and photographers. Documentary film, journalism, and the whole range of written media will be essential. Dramatic and documentary filmmakers can tell the stories of how companies use data. Fiction can inspire a deeper intellectual appreciation for data environment issues. The success of a data environmental movement will be determined by whether the fundamental concerns and ideas of data environmentalism are taken up by energetic and creative communicators and whether the movement earns sympathy from the editors, publishers, and producers who hold sway over commercial media.

Environmentalism was controversial when it began and remains controversial today. It is fiercely opposed by powerful economic interests that stand to benefit when rules are relaxed or eliminated. Legions of credentialed experts earn their daily bread by declaring the "inefficiency" of regulations. Media seeking to cover both sides of the story give credence to critics of environmentalism.

In the United States, big oil and other commercial interests have undermined any consensus about climate change, but the tide of history and common sense has risen in parallel with the actual physical tides. When it comes to the efficacy of environmental rules, it's fair to ask why a simple comparison between, say, the air quality in China and that in the United States or Western Europe hasn't ended the debate.

Yet despite the powerful forces fighting it every step of the way, environmentalism swept through the developed world. The Kyoto accords and carbon limits are scuttled for the time being, but the EPA and the broad environmental interests it represents are not going away. Despite the occasional embarrassment, environmentalism, like conservation and public safety, delivers tangible results and remains broadly popular.

Data as Property

What exactly is data? We can agree on the dictionary definition of "facts and statistics collected for reference or analysis," but that doesn't really answer the deeper question of *what*, exactly, data is. Is data a pure abstraction, merely an idea that can only exist in the human mind? Or does it have a physical nature—handwritten or printed lists, recorded sound, video, and books. What about electronic data—the chips, files, and software of the virtual world?

Those questions have an answer, of course. Data always has a physical nature. Books and vinyl records are certainly data and obviously tangible. Electronic records are also physical. Despite its complexity and seeming abstraction, on a granular scale an electronic record is a physical pattern etched, written, and electromagnetically set into a mineral or plastic or metal medium. Even the abstract ideas and memories in the human mind are really all physical items. The human brain is real and tangible and located in our skull. While its complex workings elude our full understanding, various physical regions of the brain control memory, emotion, and logic. So data, and this applies to *all* data, is not abstract. It's physical, tangible, and real. Which leads to a less obvious proposition.

If data is physical, then everything physical is *potentially* data. That's not immediately obvious. But all physical things—rocks, trees, mountains, air, even *ideas*—are constituted of specific arrangements of matter. Whether or not every arrangement of matter constitutes data is a more subtle question. The answer, literally, is in the eye of the beholder. A book can embody data measured or recorded by humans. A rock embodies data as well, but unless it was intentionally shaped or changed by some human process, the data embodied in a rock lacks a human author. A rock is a record of nature, not wholly scrutable, authored by God or, if you prefer, by the deep natural laws not made by man.

Once I touch that rock, though, it's a record of me. It becomes data. Say I take a fragment of marble and sculpt a marble bust of Homer. Assuming I acquire the marble properly, that's my rock. And it's my bust, my "art" if you are generous enough to call it that. I can sell it, I can rent it, and I can lock it away. You certainly can't just take it from me. The same is true if, after I sculpt that bust, I take a cell-phone photograph of it. My phone records the image digitally: a long string of ones and zeros electromagnetically written, "sculpted" if you will, into a circuit of metal and silicon. That digital image is mine too. You can't just take it.

The transformation that made my piece of rock into my personal "data" was intentional. What happens when I unintentionally transform a rock into something else? What if I unconsciously step on a rock and break it in two? Is that my data as well?

The answer, interestingly, is yes. Although I did not intend to break the rock, and I was wholly unconscious that my step caused the rock to break, that broken rock was caused by me. Given sufficient context, that broken rock can reveal a great number of things that I am totally unaware I just recorded in stone for others (at least potentially) to see. For one thing, the broken rock records my passage. The position of fragments indicates my direction of travel. The surface chemistry of the fracture tells something about how long it's been exposed to air, in effect recording exactly when my footstep fell. And the micro-structure of the rock and the geometry of the fracture tell something about my weight. Statistical comparison with surrounding rocks will yield tremendously more useful information. Observing which rocks shifted and which rocks shattered tells my shoe size and maybe the type and the brand of shoe. Multiple footfalls tell my rate of travel, my origin and destination, my gait, and perhaps even something about my skeletal structure and pattern of movement. Because my walking gait is unique to me, the unintentionally recorded data from a few footsteps may, assuming sufficient contextual information is available, reveal my name.

The logical extension leads to an interesting concept. Colloquially, data doesn't mean the entire physical world, the universe. In ordinary speech data is a subset of "everything." It's a physical pattern reflecting a human desire to understand, a source or basis from which knowledge can be gained. The interesting thing, though, is that knowledge can be gained from everything (and even from nothing—the spaces where things are absent). Take the rock that broke under my foot, for example. That broken rock and the ripple of cause and effect emanating from a single footstep reach to the limits of the universe. My little broken rock could (at least in theory, if the reader will allow the absurdity) lead to the cure for cancer or start a world war. As the proverb says, the wingbeat of a butterfly might cause a hurricane.

Everything affects everything else, and every element of matter is linked to a greater or lesser degree to the rest of the physical world. Every fact, then, has a physical manifestation. Each becomes an element in the ever-changing mosaic of reality. And everything—every single thing—is *data*. Data is not an abstraction. Even "virtual" data is physical. Behind every digital record is a string of zeroes and ones intricately coded into silicon, metal, plastic, or even (back in the olden days) paper. Each atom and each electron, whether racing through the transistors of a chip or calmly resting in a memory circuit, are discrete physical objects. No matter how minute, the quantum elements of data can be seen, touched, moved, and weighed. And *owned*.

Physical things, particularly items that we readily capture and put to use, are capable of being owned. Data, then, is capable of being owned. And the ownability of data is crucial. All data is *property*.

In the past, we didn't treat data that way. The small-data paradigm segmented data into two categories: the valuable and the worthless. On the one hand were the extremely valuable data sets. For example, a secret chemical formula or manufacturing process might be treated as something of great value. Access could be restricted and special care taken to avoid revealing the secret. Discrete collections of data, for example, an extensive customer list or an author's text, could also be protected. No single customer name and no single printed word had significant value on their own, but a carefully organized compilation could be very valuable. A body of law arose around secrets and original works, which were categorized as "intellectual" property.

Intellectual property gained currency as a thing of recognized value and could be bought or sold, in some cases, for large sums.

So in the small-data paradigm there was something called intellectual property, and then there was everything else. The data wake constantly emanating from our daily lives was treated as if it had no value whatsoever. The small-data paradigm didn't suppose that data could be captured and recorded on an immense scale. Single facts were seen as essentially worthless, given the lack of any practical ability to place them in any context that would make them valuable. That kind of everyday information was treated as a free but almost inaccessible resource. When information technology started to capture and collect data sets, the public was delighted by the prospect of new knowledge and new services. So far, little consideration has been given to future implications.

Meanwhile, chip manufacturers continue their relentless march along the curve of Moore's law. Implications that once seemed remote have arrived. The consequences increase geometrically, every day, around the clock. The granular intelligence of immense data sets allows a thorough knowledge of our economic system and its decision makers. Both buyers and sellers are at a profound disadvantage compared to the middleman, a data giant who knows them to the last detail and names the price to each. Big data brings with it the power to collect increasing amounts of surplus at the expense of both consumers and producers.

But that's not the way things have to be. To see alternatives, you have to develop a framework for evaluating who actually owns the data wake of an individual. It's not an easy question at first. In the small-data paradigm, what one does in public is, well, public. And what one does in a shop seems fair game for the shop to study. But that's not a valid proposition anymore. Data giants, in effect, follow us through life, recording our every step, from what we do in public to what we do in shops (or online) and even to what we do in our most private space, our home. The small-data paradigm does not consider this. The analogy would be hiring a private investigator to follow an individual, taking pictures and recording conversations, listening in on phone calls, opening mail, and sifting through garbage. It's no longer just one thing being recorded, it's everything. And that's no longer fair game, because a deep knowledge of economic actors leads to profound asymmetries in information and market power. The combination of panoptic perspective, minute observation, and indelible recording creates a formerly unimagined condition that we term *panprivity*. Panprivity refers to a state of mass observation in which a few well-capitalized organizations know virtually everything about virtually everyone, in real time, and they never forget.

Among our oldest notions of privacy is a sense of personal modesty, the same sense that makes it uncomfortable to undress in front of strangers. Yet even that most basic notion of privacy has fallen prey to the technology deployed in every airport. Formerly the subject of science fiction, millimeter wave scanners digitally undress airline passengers with ease, minutely observing and recording the contours and shape of each body. Is the naked image of our bodies not our own property? Can another person or company take that image and claim ownership of it, to be used for any purpose?

The answer should be a simple no. No, a company can't just take a picture of a naked body and sell it to someone else or use the picture for its own purposes. The unclothed image of one's body is owned by oneself. It's private. And it's property. Anyone taking a picture or making a record of such an intimate image is stealing, unless he or she has permission to do so.

Do the data giants have permission? They would certainly say yes. In their analysis, taking a picture or recording user data does not involve the transfer of property. Companies say, in effect, that the data they collect is of their own creation. That's a bit misleading, though. If you took an unauthorized picture—a photocopy, for example—of a document detailing the private affairs of a company, you would surely risk a lawsuit for something akin to theft. Companies and governments take enormous precautions to protect their data. Imagine trying to access the "personal" data of Amazon or Facebook or Google. Good luck getting access, but if you were clever enough to get into the system, you should expect a barrage of lawsuits accusing you of stealing. So why should a different rule apply to individuals? Clearly we each have private data, "intellectual property" if you will call it that. A data giant shouldn't be able to copy our intellectual property and claim it as its own.

Isn't a panprivitous record of our lives even more revealing than a naked image? After all, it contains tremendously intimate information about us. Is it reasonable to take issue with a company that captures our nude images but be perfectly comfortable with a company that makes a movie with a complete database of our lives, recording every place we go, what we do, what we write, and who we interact with? The more or less obvious conclusion has to be that a data wake is (1) property, (2) private, and (3) owned by the individual it intimately depicts. That means all your personal data doesn't belong to a data giant. It belongs to you. When a company records your private information and claims ownership, it steals your property. There's an urgent need for a new understanding of the totality of our personal data. The public must demand that personal data be treated as personal property, not free game for a company to record, declare a corporate asset, and place beyond the individual's control.

10

Resuscitating the Consumer

So far as the public can see, big data's influence on commerce seems almost trivial: targeted web advertising. After viewing televisions for sale on the web, for the next day or two consumers repeatedly see online advertisements for televisions. Although the technology behind that process is actually quite interesting, the result is pretty disappointing. The ads are "relevant" in a purely mechanical sense, but they don't demonstrate much intelligence. There's no recognition that customers who actually buy products that are neither collectors' items nor frequently replaced—for example, a television—might not be in the market for another right after making a purchase. Despite the promise and potential of big data, the results so far seem fairly benign. Advertisers can't even distinguish who has just bought something from who hasn't.

Several factors work to limit the consumer-surplus gold rush. The sheer scale of the data available can be difficult to manage. Separating signal from noise remains as much art as science. When Google first publicized its Flu Trends project, it drew a flurry of attention from an audience eager to hear about the predictive powers of big data. Google's 2008 paper in the science journal *Nature* described a 90 percent correlation between forty-five search terms and a proxy measure for ensuing influenza cases in the relevant region. The results were stunning. Google offered a tantalizing glimpse of how big-data analytics could answer seemingly impossible questions accurately, effortlessly, and in real time. There was just one thing: It didn't really work. The next few years showed that the techniques the Flu Trends team used are no more reliable than traditional "small-data" predictive methods. To the disappointment of many, we still lack concrete, publicly verifiable evidence that analyzing large amorphous data sets can produce extraordinary results.

The complexity of comparing data from different sources remains a daunting challenge. Google Flu Trends used what was already at hand: a granular, real-time feed of Google searches entered by millions of users. But the data universe is far larger than that. The total pool of data available from all sources is many times bigger than Google's search-term feed, but that data is stored in inconsistent formats and offers varying degrees of precision. Take consumer surveys, for example. Surveys represent a rich source of personal data, but they are not easily correlated with the rest of the data world. Consumer names, for example, are typically not unique. Date and time may be vague. Self-descriptive information can be ambiguous, misspelled, oddly worded, corrupted, irrelevant, or even, as is often the case, a lie.

In practice, data scientists find themselves spending a large portion of their time "cleaning" data sets for further analysis. Duplicate, erroneous, and spurious data is removed or corrected, and formats are harmonized in what can be a painstaking process. The irony is rich. In the current state of data science, in order to take advantage of the awesome power of analytic machines, a lot of prep work still must be done by hand. Intensive effort is required, involving craftsmanlike skill. The best data scientists are still, essentially, artisans and artists.

And there's a more fundamental problem. Data, after all, is a record of the past. Even real-time data must occur at least an instant before it can be sensed and recorded. Careful observation of any historical record can lead to important insights. Or, as is often the case, it can lead to misconceptions. As statisticians say, correlation is not causation. Causation, the deep knowledge we desire, is a tricky subject indeed.

Humans possess an innate capacity to understand the causes of things. It begins from birth, and it's both sophisticated and reasonably accurate. As a practical matter, our conception of cause is extremely useful. Individual lives and whole societies are built on accepted assumptions about causative relationships. Gravity causes objects to fall. Jokes cause people to smile.

Yet at a deep level, cause is never completely known. One doesn't doubt gravity. A belief in gravity is as sure as knowledge gets. But that doesn't mean anybody really understands the causative mechanism involved. It's easy to say that a mystical force called "gravity" caused Newton's apple to fall from bough to earth. It's not so easy to say what gravity is, what gravity is made of, how it acts at a distance, or what causes gravity itself. Those answers elude our greatest minds. Instead, we continue with everyday life, observing what throughout human history has been a perfect correlation: When dropped, stuff falls. Every time.

Still, even gravity hovers somewhere just shy of empirical certainty. We can't, after all, isolate gravity using the scientific method to compare a test tube full of gravity to one without. We just keep dropping apples and, at least so far, they keep falling.

Systems involving human behavior—buying and selling, say, or economic growth—are far more complex than the force of gravity. And like gravity, human behavior can't be fully explained. So many factors complicate human behavior that our knowledge of it tends to be experiential rather than experimental. It's not practical to conduct controlled experiments on people using the scientific method. Instead, we study our experience. That means we study history, in particular historic correlations. Virtually all of our knowledge of human behavior comes from observing historic correlations rather than from scientific experimentation.

Do we understand the causes of human behavior or the causes of economic performance? Throughout history, humans have gained experience and drawn conclusions. But finding a historic correlation between any two things doesn't reveal the cause. The ground is always wet when it rains, but one shouldn't think the wet ground causes rain to fall. Unemployment rises during recessions, but that doesn't mean unemployment causes recessions.

Big data suffers from fundamental limitations. Predicting future events is hard. Things that haven't happened yet aren't data, so they can't be studied. The historical record provides lots of resources for predicting future events but no perfect ones. New phenomena have a habit of cropping up that can't be anticipated by studying the past.

It's naïve, though, to think that big data's limitations will keep its eventual impact small. One of data's interesting features is that as its quantity increases, the knowledge that can be derived from that data increases even more quickly. We may not be able to explain gravity or explain why a consumer buys toothpaste. But when we electronically watch millions of apples fall in real time or millions of consumers buy toothpaste, we gain a depth of knowledge beyond the ordinary human powers of observation. Putting each tube of toothpaste into context, siting it within a specific place and time in the data universe—the panoptic record of everything else existing or occurring at the same time—can render insights that are very deep indeed. Given sufficient data and computational power, the mysteries of causation become mere statistical problems. Over time they can be solved.

What's more, technology steadily improves. With more and more data to choose from and more computational resources to draw from, answers that once were unobtainable will eventually become readily available. If current trends continue, it's only a matter of time before data giants gain extraordinary knowledge from the data they are collecting. Of course, current trends are never certain, and Moore's law can't hold forever. Physicists speculate about the limits of data processing. The so-called Bekenstein bound postulates an upper limit on the computing power that will fit into the universe. We are, of course, nowhere near that bound, and we can't even be sure it exists. But big data certainly has practical limitations. Data isn't infinite. Truly panoptic sensors don't exist. Not all systems communicate. And the number of computer chips available to work on a given calculation, although very large, is limited.

So the question is, what should we expect? Should we believe that the limitations of data science will forever overwhelm its seemingly magical potential or that data science will ultimately, perhaps soon, prevail in answering formerly intractable questions? This book's task isn't to offer a rigorous answer on that fundamental point. Rather, our ambition is to offer a persuasive answer. And that very concept, the distinction between a complete answer and one that's good enough, is key to understanding why data science will, in fact, produce extraordinary results. The benefits of data science will derive from fabulously expensive systems available only to large organizations, and those results will change the nature of markets forever.

To capture an increasing share of consumer surplus, the data giant doesn't have to perfectly understand the deep causes of human behavior. All the data giant needs is an edge. Like players in a casino, consumers will gamble against the house, and the house will set the rules to its advantage. It's okay if somebody "wins," getting an extra discount or a particularly good deal. That's just part of the game. Because on average, little by little, the house wins. The house's edge is statistical rather than absolute.

We know that the data feed into the data giants is very rich. We know that if that data were delivered into the hands of a skilled investigator, the investigator could derive commercially valuable information about an individual from the feed. Automating the process of investigation is eminently possible, and it's being done right now. What's more, the science gets better all the time.

Which brings us to the final question: When? Assume for a moment that everyone accepts that data science will produce extraordinary results, and that those results will (absent any countervailing change) consign mass markets to the ash heap of history. Both of those propositions could be perfectly true yet of little present significance if the rate of improvement in data science unfolds over centuries. If one accepts that we face a big issue, how urgent is it?

Consider the following thought experiment. Suppose for a moment that Moore's law broke right now, and there could be no further advances in electronics. All further growth in data and computing power would be a matter of linear change, building more capacity using tools already in existence. Can there be a doubt that already, today, the data feed is rich enough to provide an extremely valuable "edge" to a data giant? That feed already includes our physical locations, our written and phone communications, our web histories, our online and offline transaction histories, and innumerable other historical facts and observations. It seems plain that the data feed is already rich enough to threaten at least a portion of the consumer surplus.

But is the computational power available now? That's a tougher question. A lot of computing power is available, but the consumer surplus presents a very large computational challenge. Large as the challenge is, it doesn't seem insurmountable. Consider the following: A highly reliable (although imperfect) indicator of wealth and income is one's home. Estimated home values in much of the world are well established and readily accessible online, albeit without perfect accuracy. Consumer identities and addresses are also readily available to data giants. It is almost a trivial exercise to connect the home to the person, thereby creating a database, admittedly imperfect but still highly useful, reflecting the means of nearly all consumers. That information alone can be sufficient input to fuel an intelligent, real-time price engine that extracts additional value from people who are believed to have greater means. There may be individual glitches, of course. Warren Buffet (who lives in a normal house) might not be charged as much as he would be willing to pay for one of the hamburgers he loves. The live-in maid at a Beverly Hills address might not like what she sees when she is shown luxury products at prices intended for a movie star. But on average, most people willingly pay a premium for whatever they buy if it correlates reasonably well to their wealth, merely for the convenience of not having to shop around. They might even be well aware they are paying more, but many will accept what is to them a modest cost, rather than spend valuable time seeking alternatives.

From the data giant's perspective, capturing more consumer surplus isn't an intractable problem. The limitations are practical rather than theoretical. It will take better software and more experience, but it won't require fundamental breakthroughs or futuristic technology. And here's the important thing: Moore's law hasn't collapsed yet, and it might not for some time longer. Large players already have all the tools to begin chipping away at the economy's surplus right now: money, brains, and physical assets. Their capability to collect and use data continues to expand geometrically. So we think there is an answer to the last question, the question of "when." The answer is right now.

So far, we haven't addressed one other limit on the data giants. In a sense, it's the subject of this book. That's because the other limit on the relentless progress of data science is you. Large-scale data collection requires the willing participation of millions of consumers. For better or worse, consumers have eagerly cooperated up to this point. But their cooperation has been obtained by manipulative means. "Free" services such as e-mail, search, and social networking must provide sufficient value for consumers to use them. That's a given, because those services offer real benefits. But as economists like to say, there's no such thing as a free lunch. An exchange is involved that the data giant is not up front about. In exchange for the service, the data giant gets your data and a license to exploit it.

Most of the biggest web services started out "free." Short of paying people to use a service, "free" is as compelling as it gets. But keep in mind that users don't get all the benefits of e-mail, search, and social networking without paying. They just don't pay in money, at least not in a straightforward exchange. They pay in data, a valuable asset that, in effect, can be redeemed later on by a data giant, again and again. The largest consumer Internet services are built on a debt-like model. Facebook provides a service, and in effect, you borrow the price from them by paying in data. Facebook then takes your data and, through the alchemy of data science, redeems the debt by collecting some surplus from you over time, making a tidy profit along the way. So users do pay after all. It's just hard to tell how much. Consider, though, that even though Facebook doesn't make as much money as some other companies, investors think it is worth an enormous sum. If the investors are correct, the stock value is going to come from somewhere. The somewhere is you. And data is how. It's interesting that companies call consumers "users." One might stop and consider who, exactly, is the user and who is used.

Once web giants lure consumers in, the cost and hassle of switching increases all the time. Eventually the service providers wind up with captive, dependent users who don't require a high level of service. To get users to switch, any competitor will have to provide significantly more value. That's always possible, of course. But in addition to their market position, the wealth and resources of data giants like Google and Facebook are formidable obstacles. Rather than face competition from new upstarts, data giants spend billions buying up potential competitors. Their scale gives them tremendous advantages.

The options for consumers are not particularly attractive. Consumer user agreements are not exactly negotiable. Web services are a take-it-or-leave-it proposition, and in an increasingly networked world, leaving the network is not a great option. And in any case, a customer leaving Facebook, for example, isn't usually leaving the

Internet. She's just moving from the clutches of one data giant to another.

Some services promise a degree of anonymity, a potential defense against the wholesale capture of data. It's a nice idea, but it's no solution. True anonymity online is a practical impossibility. Even services like Tor that have devised clever protections for web communications are susceptible to certain kinds of attacks. And like any organization, Tor is susceptible to infiltration or top-down influence despite the pains it takes to assure the public that it does not share data with other interested parties. In the age of Edward Snowden, it's hard to take such assurances at face value.

More fundamentally, though, web anonymity just doesn't work. A sufficient number of external sensors and data sources provide rich context about consumers even without access to any web content. And you can't run your whole online life through Tor or a similar service. Sooner or later you're going to buy something from Amazon. Retailers will increasingly push transactions onto the Internet in order to take advantage of real-time pricing opportunities. The key point is that given sufficient context, almost anything you do or buy can reveal important data about you, whether online or off.

The better path is consumer empowerment. Certainty of ownership is essential. In Chapter 9 we compared granular personal data with nude photographs and concluded that personal data is owned by the individual, not the data repository. Consumers should speak up for their rights, not stand mute as data giants blatantly expropriate their private property. For starters, consumers can demand full access to their data held by others. Going further, consumers can demand meaningful boundaries on the commercial use of their data and ask for the removal of personal data when they no longer wish to permit a company to use it. If sufficient numbers of customers demand data reforms, a grassroots movement to limit the depredations of data giants can succeed.

Some Fine Print of Our Own

Try another thought experiment. Suppose a housecleaning company offered to clean your house for free. The proposal is very innovative because they won't use people. They will send robots into your house who will do a number of cleaning chores. You'd probably like to try it for the novelty if nothing else, but who knows, it might be a great service. And it's free, right? So the next thing that happens is a robot showing up at your door and announcing it's ready to go to work. Just one thing, though, before it starts. You have to click through the user agreement. Which is twenty pages long. Of course, you click "accept" and you don't read it because no one ever reads that stuff—life is too short. If you had read it, in addition to a lot of other terms the user agreement would have informed you, "We will use information we obtain concerning the interior of your home and its contents to provide our services, to maintain and improve our services, and to develop new services. We will not share your personally identifiable information without your consent." That's familiar language; most people wouldn't object.

But maybe they should. Because in this thought experiment, here's what that robot does. First of all, it's really helpful. It does your cleaning really well, and it doesn't complain or ask for money. You hardly even notice that it begins to shadow you at home, even anticipating whether you need a glass of water or a cup of tea. Then, after you are hooked, the robot starts to talk to you. It starts offering you products and telling you about things you might want to buy. The creepy thing is that the robot knows you so well. It knows when your socks have holes in them and tries to sell you socks. It knows when you are down to just peanut butter and jelly and tries to sell you sushi from the great restaurant that just opened. It's really good at selling, and you start to get used to that too. Eventually, you begin letting the robot tell you what to do.

Is this beginning to sound familiar? It should, because if you use Google Search or Hotmail or Facebook, that's exactly what is going on. A data giant is collecting tons of data about you on terms that you don't even understand. The user agreement you signed literally doesn't mean a thing. The data giant can spy on you as much as it wants and then do whatever it wants with your personal data. There's no restriction, no limit whatsoever.

Consumers need to realize that they don't have to accept the data giant's rules. The user agreements, technically known as contracts of adhesion, are so flimsy that it's doubtful they are even remotely enforceable. The tricky wording that sounds so reasonable and safe seems intentionally misleading, perhaps forming a plausible basis for charging data giants with fraud. It's foreseeable, perhaps even likely, that consumers have valid legal claims against the data giants for misappropriation of their personal intellectual property, invasion of their personal privacy, unauthorized exploitation of personal identity, and other well-recognized wrongs under current U.S. law. The problem is—and the data giants are well aware of this—you can readily prove that a data giant has done something wrong, but you simply lack the data to figure out exactly what the harm was. You can't tell how much the data giant is costing you because only the data giant knows that—and it's not saying.

Government regulation has been a sad failure. In the United States, it's practically nonexistent. The Federal Communications Commission, the Federal Trade Commission, and the Department of Justice have been culpably negligent, lifting nary a finger to address the laughable state of user agreements. It's a different situation in Europe. Well-intentioned consumer protection regulations have been proposed in Europe, for example, limiting the use of vague user agreements and requiring the deletion of personal data upon request. The trouble is, although regulation is certainly part of the solution, it can't be all of the solution. Regulators who focus on mandating corporate behavior are doomed to fail. When the European Union puts certain categories or techniques of data use off-limits, it doesn't take long for data giants to figure out a work-around. Technique-oriented regulation is always doomed because of the fundamental nature of big data and data science. Given sufficient data, fast-adapting intelligence engines can indirectly achieve any objective that is directly prohibited. Using the huge data sets that now make up big data allows so many ways to "skin the cat" that prohibiting specific activities will always fall behind the curve. Regulation of technique can never catch up to the cutting edge of technology. So while U.S. regulators (and the officials to whom they report) have largely left consumers to fend for themselves, they may have done the American public a favor by failing to lull Americans into believing they are protected. Europeans should take approximately zero comfort in the actions (at least so far) of their regulators.

That's not to say that regulation has no place in the data economy. Issues such as equal access to the public network, the absolute privacy of messages, photos and phone conversations, and fair terms for user agreements are areas ripe for regulatory focus. But these, while important, will not solve the underlying commercial problem. Data giants can still thrive despite net neutrality, better privacy protections, and less onerous user agreements. The worst behavior can be restricted, but ultimately public utility and antitrust laws will be essential to maintain the fairness of markets. Unfortunately, antitrust by its very nature always comes too late because it generally doesn't come into play until somebody has already accumulated a great deal of power.

Several existing legal rules could be brought into play. The right to privacy and the guaranteed ownership of the commercial value of one's identity are well-recognized principles. It's plausible that enlightened judges would accept arguments based on these principles to limit data exploitation. There is some groundwork to do first, though. The right of privacy itself originated with a scholarly article in the *Harvard Law Review*. The prestige of that publication and the authors' persuasive arguments gave sufficient cover to judges who were sympathetic with privacy concerns in the newspaper age (an advanced technology at the time) to rule against firms that exploited private information for profit.

Another legal doctrine already on the books, the law of fiduciary responsibility, may hold even more promise in achieving a more benign balance of power among the data giants and consumers. In some areas, particularly in the investment field, persons entrust property of great value to agents who manage it on behalf of the owners. The legal doctrine of fiduciary duty requires the agent in whom so much trust is placed to act with integrity in protecting the client's interest and to steer clear of making money at the client's expense without full disclosure and genuine consent. The concept is an equitable one with a long history in our law. It would be no great stretch to apply the fiduciary protections familiar in the investment context to cover aggregations of personal data. The real specter of liability for fiduciary breaches could be a significant incentive to behave responsibly and to put consumer interests first.

More controversial than regulation, but still potentially useful, is the class-action lawsuit. Making the case that a wrong has occurred is the easy part. The tough part is figuring out the consequences. Search engines and e-mail and social networks really do wonderful things for customers. Concrete harms are hard to identify, at least so far. It's even possible that significant harms don't yet exist. Of course, the data giants aren't about to open their doors to researchers looking for evidence of consumer harm, and it would take quite an investment to sift through the facts. That last issue—the expertise and investment needed just to figure out what data giants are doing—is probably fatal to class actions for now. It's one thing to spend some legal time on a speculative claim. But nobody is going to invest what it takes to hoist the data giants on their own petard. There's just too much cost involved.

It's possible that antitrust and utility rules may be the only way to slow the gold rush. The single existential threat to data giants (besides technical obsolescence) is government control through antitrust or public utility regulation. Companies like Google and Facebook are vulnerable to lawmakers who put boundaries on their methods and their size. It's troubling, though, that today the most significant competitors to the U.S.-based Internet giants are other national governments jealous of the data-derived power held by American companies (and the U.S. government). With the sometimes grudging assistance of data giants like Google and Verizon, the United States (and it is hardly alone) has been collecting vast amounts of data not ostensibly for commercial reasons but to project geopolitical power beyond its borders. That leaves the United States and other governments deeply conflicted about matters of privacy. Institutional or personal jealousy over the inherent power of knowledge may provide other motives for regulators to act. In the world's advanced democracies, it will ultimately be up to the people to insist on the protections necessary to preserve the consumer surplus and with it, the free market. Political officials may follow, but they should not be expected to lead, at least not without lots of help.

Meanwhile every potential abuse foretold in this book has actually already occurred, albeit sometimes in a crude or preliminary form. No sector of the economy is immune to the temptation to exploit consumers. Some U.S. doctors—probably our most trusted professionals, the same people who pledge to "do no harm"—make a practice of abusively billing emergency-room patients, arguably the most vulnerable customers imaginable. Google, a much admired company, admits to reading our e-mail for its own purposes. Airlines in whom the flying public places immense trust offer different pricing from moment to moment based on data, and for reasons, known only to them. Throughout the economy, advertising is tailored to who databases say we are. And mass-market pricing has already splintered into a complex game.

We know that the market, left to itself, won't deliver solutions that limit the advantages of data giants. Disappearing messages (do they really disappear?) and Internet sites that don't track you (are you really anonymous?) are well and good in theory, but they don't work in practice. Looking for entrepreneurs to solve the data-exploitation problem is foolish. Profit-driven solutions are not the answer because the profit itself is the problem. Technical solutions will never be powerful enough on their own to tip the scales against the data giants. Collective action is essential.

And the collective action that works will have to use the tools at hand. Fortunately, a powerful tool is readily available. There are two existing legal doctrines that, creatively applied, can effect highly beneficial changes. They have an ancient and unquestioned pedigree, lying near the heart of our commercial society since its beginning. The first is the law of property, and the second is the law of contract. We have already touched on the subject of property. Personal data, particularly intimate, extensive, panoptic data, is a physical reality. Data is touchable and ownable. And it seems unarguable that deeply identifying personal data, the granular portraits of our lives and personalities made possible by big data, is owned by the individual it relates to. That data can be sold or rented or regulated according to personal choice. And that's where the law of contract comes in. Individuals can contractually control the use of their data. It's an obvious conclusion, if you think about it. The very existence of user "agreements" tacitly acknowledges that there is something—which can only be property— to be agreed upon. Each data giant's terms of service implicitly admit that the data is property belonging to the individual, and the individual can enter into a binding contract relating to it.

So here's a modest proposal: Why don't we do that? By binding contract, we are not referring to the typical user agreement. Besides the

216 ALL YOU CAN PAY

fact that it takes a little effort and organizing to write a good contract and roll it out on a scale for mass adoption, why don't consumers start telling the Facebooks of the world about their own terms of service? It's an important principle that consumers should call the shots when it comes to their own data, so there should probably be many different versions. But here are a few terms that a consumer ought to require.

When we interact with a data giant, we generally do so through a device. And usually, though not always, that device belongs to us. In the robot-housecleaner analogy, our smartphone or tablet or laptop is the house. When we access a web service on our device, the data giant, in effect, sends a robot into our house to do stuff. That robot should stick to what it's supposed to do and not hang around taking pictures of everything in the house, listening to everything we say, watching everything we do, and reporting it in real time. That robot shouldn't interrupt us in the middle of something else with commercial offers and should only make offers we permit in advance. When we share some private stuff with the robot, for example, our mail, the robot should keep it secret and not use it for any purpose. The robot should forget things after a little while, or at least remember them only at our request. And most of all, we should retain ownership and control of our data because it is our property.

All that's needed is a website where consumers can make more informed choices about their property and, perhaps with a little prompting, generate a personal user agreement tailored just for them. Those user agreements could then be rolled out on a mass scale to web companies, who could take or leave them. Suddenly, we'd have a whole new ball game. Big-brother companies that tell us not to worry—they only want to help—but that don't address personal data issues in an up-front way would begin to feel pushback. To win commercially, companies would have to adapt to more equal terms between the selling entity and the consumer and continue to stay current as consumer privacy preferences change. The premise should no longer be "agree to the company's user agreement or keep out." The premise should be: Accept the consumer's terms or leave her alone. We need companies trained to respond to consumers, not the other way around.

The Role of Government

It's ironic that in many ways the Internet owes its existence to government, because most web business leaders passionately desire to keep the government from getting involved with Internet commerce. The funny thing is, they don't see the crucial role that government already plays. The debate over Internet neutrality is an excellent example. Among the most hotly contested regulatory issues relating to the Internet, the neutrality principle requires the companies that operate the Internet to charge all customers the same price for access. The irony is that the only thing protecting many Internet businesses from the depredations of data giants, particularly infrastructure behemoths like Verizon and AT&T, is government regulation. For years the government required the big telecom companies to carry traffic on a nondiscriminatory basis. They weren't allowed to charge different prices to different customers, whether based on volume or otherwise. There was one price for all.

Verizon and AT&T, of course, know they can make more money if they can tailor pricing to each customer. Analogous to the consumer surplus, it's the producer surplus that's at stake in the net neutrality debate. The telcos can make pretty good guesses at how much companies will pay to use the necessary data pipelines, and if they are allowed to, they will set prices right at the maximum for each company. What's more, they can use airline-style fast-pricing systems in which prices shift from moment to moment at the whim of the telecom firms. It's interesting that so many Internet entrepreneurs are jumping up and down saying that variable pricing is, if not inherently wrong, at least unfair.

Would they, though, support the regulation of consumer pricing to maintain both transparent terms and uniform pricing in commodity markets? They should, because unless you want to live in a hyper-Darwinian winner-take-all society, you should support commodity markets. We all love to choose among the tremendous variety of products and services available today, but the business ecosystems that enable all that wonderful diversity depend on commodity markets with transparent, uniform, and predictable pricing. Basic inputs like water and electricity (and telecom services!) are terrible candidates for splintering up into complex and fast-moving speculative markets. We want variety in the marketplace, but to get that, we must create and protect a viable space for entrepreneurs and small businesses that do things differently or in new ways. If narrow private interests take control of commodity markets, in addition to directly threatening both the consumer and the producer surplus, the ensuing price instability will require startups to occur only within economic fiefdoms big enough and rich enough to protect a new venture until it can stand on its own. The ranks of owners will shrink in number and increase in wealth as entrepreneurs become just another kind of employee.

So despite all the vocalizing to the contrary, government plays a role after all. Government has to promote the common good by limiting the exploitation of monopoly power through public utility-type regulation. Fast pricing, with flash boys trading electricity, water, oil, and data with hopelessly outgunned consumers and small businesses, should be tamped down. Government should facilitate a framework for forming mutually beneficial user agreements. And government should take steps to ensure that surplus-creating mass markets continue to exist.

Business has a role. All but the biggest businesses remain vulnerable to data giants seeking to capture producer surplus. Rather than taking a knee-jerk stance against regulation, businesses should recognize the parallel between their desire for net neutrality and similar consumers' needs. Those who fear the deadening effects of government regulations, admittedly a legitimate concern, should at least have the intellectual honesty to admit that private monopolies can have the same regulating and deadening effects. Business, at least those businesses that aren't data giants or data-giant wannabes, should join forces with the consumer data environmentalism movement rather than oppose it. And consumers should support a diverse, dynamic, and entrepreneurial economy. A dynamic, free, innovative economy results from a balance of forces rather than dominance by giant monopolies.

Government is essential, but it isn't going to magically make everything okay. Like the natural environmental movement, the data environmental movement has to start with committed individuals and then grow into groups, national organizations, and ultimately, a global movement. Writers, artists, and filmmakers have a role to play in imagining the world we want to live in and depicting the outcomes to avoid. Effort and patience are required.

We don't have another century to get ready. The imperatives of technology are more urgent than ever. The data environmental movement needs to start acting now, today, to build the world we want to live in and leave for our children. The focus must shift to creating lasting value rather than gaming customers for profit. Government can address the things we formally decide to do together. If we build a data environmental movement, the requisite government will follow. The tools are at hand. All we need to do is use them.

Your Own Terms

Every day, consumers are asked to "agree" to densely-written terms and conditions covering personal data and privacy that they have little chance of reading and virtually no chance of fully comprehending. What if, instead of blindly clicking through all those "I agree" and "Accept" buttons and then hoping for the best, consumers had a way to establish a few terms of their own to apply to all companies doing business with them?

The website myuseragreement.com offers individual users an opportunity to regain ownership of their digital selves. Participants can select from a menu of options to write their own personal contractual terms for the ownership and use of their personal data. Behind the scenes, the website will communicate individual preferences to major service providers such as Google, Microsoft, Yahoo, and Facebook, and is positioned to put all internet companies on notice that participants have established their own personal terms of service.

Acknowledgments

We are grateful for the contributions, large and small, of many people around the world who assisted us during the creation of this book. Several deserve special thanks. Our good friend and agent, John Thornton, provided steady guidance at every step. Without his advocacy, this book would not exist. John has remarkable insight into all things literary and also happens to be an incredible human being. We are undeserving beneficiaries of his intelligence and professionalism. The entire publishing team at Nation Books has been a pleasure to work with, but we could not fail to specially mention the contributions of Clive Priddle, Carl Bromley, and Dan LoPreto, whose belief in our ideas made this book possible. Our fabulous editor Alessandra Bastagli applied a sure hand exactly where needed. Her calm, efficient, and encouraging support has been greatly appreciated. Tania and Laurie Crockett, Miloslav and Alexandra Bernasek, and Mary Jo and the late Larry Mongan each deserve thanks for their guidance and inspiration. And finally we thank our most attentive audience of all, Lily and Natalie, whose love and understanding give us both pleasure and purpose.

The authors alone are responsible for any deficiency in this book. The views and opinions expressed herein are solely those of the authors and do not represent the views or opinions of their respective employers or clients or of any other person, organization, or entity.

Notes on Sources

Introduction

Our little fable owes its shape to Rachel Carson's *Silent Spring*, published in 1962 by Houghton Mifflin Company. Her book opens with a similar passage titled "A Fable for Tomorrow."

Chapter 1

In retelling the story of the launch of Perrier, we rely on an interview with Bruce Nevins as well as other sources, including an article by Kristin McMurran called "The New Story of Eau: Businessman Bruce Nevins Persuades America to Order 'Perrier, Please,'" published in *People*, June 26, 1978; and "Must Be Something in the Water" by Julia Moskin, published February 15, 2006, in the *New York Times*; and the Perrier website, which describes the company's history. Our statistics on bottled-water consumption and beverage consumption come from *The Beverage Information Group 2013 Handbook*, a study called *Bottled Water in the US, 2013* from the Beverage Marketing Corporation, and a study by the Nielsen Company, released in February 2014, on beverage consumption in the New York metro area. The American Water Works Association report titled *Buried No Longer: Confronting America's Water Infrastructure Challenge* from 2012 provided useful data on the cost of water. A BBC website article, "Coke's Water Bomb" by Bill Garrett, on its website on June 16, 2004, provided insight into Coke's launch of bottled water in the United Kingdom. For the consumer surplus, we corresponded with economist Hal Varian, and we interviewed Steve Pressman, an economist from Monmouth University. We also relied on Pressman's book *Fifty Major Economists*, published in paperback by Routledge in 2013. We also refer to Alfred Marshall's book *Principles of Economics,* 8th edition, published in 1920 by Macmillan and Co. The quote from "General" Robert Wood Johnson Jr. was found in Jerry Oppenheimer's book *Crazy Rich: Power, Scandal, and Tragedy Inside the Johnson & Johnson Dynasty,* published in 2013 by Macmillan.

Chapter 2

In retelling the story of how GM beat Ford, we relied heavily on work by David Gartman called "Tough Guys and Pretty Boys: The Cultural Antagonisms of Engineering and Aesthetics in Automotive History," published in 2004 on the website Automobile in American Life and Society. In telling the story of kopi luwak, we relied on our interviews with Tony Wild. In referring to aspects of the coffee market, we relied on articles, including "Where to Find Serious Coffee in New York: Everywhere" by Oliver Strand, published in the *New York Times* on May 6, 2014; and "American Workers Spend $100 on Coffee, $2000 on Lunch," published by the *Huffington Post* on January 20, 2012. Much of the data on prices on everything from coffee to medical procedures came from our own reporting. Our understanding of international cell-phone comparisons was derived from a 2010 report from the New America Foundation called *An International Comparison of Cell Phone Plans and Prices* by Chiehyu Li and Bincy Ninan-Moses, as well as our interview with Sascha Meinrath, a director of the Open Technology Institute at the New America Foundation.

Chapter 3

In describing Google's policy on Gmail, we relied on the company's own press releases and public information. For experiments with privacy, we relied on a blog post by High Tech Bridge, "Social Networks: Can Robots Violate User Privacy?" published August 27, 2013. News articles were important to our understanding of privacy issues on the web, and we relied on the following: "Test Reveals Facebook, Twitter and Google Snoop on Emails: Study of New Giants Spurs New Privacy Concerns," published in the *Daily Mail* on August 31, 2013, by Martin Delgado; "The Information Google Doesn't Want You to Organize," published on September 4, 2014, in *USA Today* by Thomas R. Burke and Jonathan Segal; and "Google: Don't Expect Privacy When Sending to Gmail" by Dominic Rushe in the *Guardian,* August 15, 2013. We quote data on e-mail and search usage from *Email Statistics Report 2013–2017,* produced by The Radicati Group

Inc. as well as *U.S. Search Engine Rankings*, released September 17, 2014, by com-Score. Original reporting on Gmail by Anna Bernasek was later published in *Newsweek* on June 25, 2014, and titled "Encryption Protects Gmail from Everyone Except Google." In order to understand Google, we read various books on the company but quoted at times directly from John Battelle's *The Search: How Google and Its Rivals Rewrote the Rules of Business and Transformed Our Culture*, published in 2005 by Portfolio. We also relied on Google's own website for company information. The *Stanford Encyclopedia of Philosophy*'s (2012) "Search Engines and Ethics," published August 27, 2012, was also an important resource for this chapter, as well as press releases from the European Commission about Google and competition concerns from 2013. Various research studies also helped inform our understanding, including *Data Brokers: A Call for Transparency and Accountability*, released by the Federal Trade Commission in 2014; "Unleashing the Value of Advanced Analytics in Insurance" by Richard Clarke and Ari Libarikian in August 2014 for McKinsey & Company's *Insights and Publications*; and "Experimental Evidence of Massive-scale Emotional Contagion Through Social Networks" by Adam D. I. Kramer, Jamie E. Guillory, and Jeffrey T. Hancock, June 17, 2014, in *Proc Natl Acad Sci USA*, issue 24. There were many news articles that we either referred to or relied on for understanding, including: "Google Unveils Ambitious Android Expansion at I/O Conference" by Brian X. Chen, the *New York Times*, June 25, 2014; "Are the Robots About to Rise? Google's New Director of Engineering Thinks So . . ." by Carole Cadwalladr in the *Guardian*, February 22, 2014; "How Companies Learn Your Secrets" by Charles Duhigg, February 16, 2012, the *New York Times*; "OKCupid: We Experiment on Users, Everyone Does" by Alex Hern in the *Guardian*, July 29, 2014; "GM's Engine Charlie Learned to Live with a Misquote" by Justin Hyde, *Detroit Free Press*, September 14, 2008; "Facebook Experiment Has Few Limits" by Reed Albergotti, the *Wall Street Journal*, July 2, 2014; and "Google Flu Trends: The Limits of Big Data" by Steve Lohr, the *New York Times*, 2014.

Chapter 4

For our understanding of how college financial aid is determined and how it evolved, we relied on a paper produced by the College Board called "A History of Needs Analysis." All data on the cost of college was sourced from the National Center for Education Statistics as well as college websites, like Harvard and Princeton, that advertise their list prices. For an insight into John

Monro, we relied on a piece in the *Harvard Magazine* by Toni-Lee Capossela and Monro's obituary in the *New York Times* on April 3, 2002. Various articles informed our understanding of price discrimination in practice, including "How Loyalty Programs Influence the Way You Shop" by Candice Choi in the AP, May 16, 2013; "Websites Vary Prices, Deals Based on Users' Information" by Jennifer Valentino-DeVries, Jeremy Singer-Vine, and Ashkan Soltani, in the *Wall Street Journal*, December 24, 2012; and "Web Sites Change Prices Based on Customers' Habits" by Anita Ramasastry, CNN, June 14, 2005. We also refer to a number of academic papers and studies, including *2013 Comparative Price Report: Variation in Medical and Hospital Prices by Country*, the International Federation of Health Plans; "Zero Defections: Quality Comes to Services" by Frederick F. Reichheld and W. Earl Sasser Jr., *Harvard Business Review*: September 1990; "The Rising Cost of College: Tuition, Financial Aid, and Price Discrimination" by Scott A. Wolla, senior economic education specialist, the Federal Reserve Bank of St. Louis, January 2014 newsletter; and "First Degree Price Discrimination Using Big Data" by Benjamin Reed Shiller, Economics Department, Brandeis University, working paper, August 20, 2013. An interview we conducted with Steve Pressman, economics professor at Monmouth University, was also important to our understanding of price discrimination.

Chapter 5

Comments by Google employees about changes to search can be found on the Official Google Blog. We found comments by Craig Silverstein about the personalization of search on a blog post called Geeking with Greg, posted May 10, 2004. We gained insight into experiments done by DuckDuckGo on Google Search from the company's press releases, as well as an article by Carl Franzen, "Google Results Are More Personalized than You Realize," posted on TPM's website, October 15, 2012. Eli Pariser's book *The Filter Bubble: How the New Personalized Web Is Changing What We Read and How We Think*, April 24, 2012, was an important source of background material. We refer to a number of research papers, including "The Anatomy of a Large-Scale Hypertextual Web Search Engine" by Sergey Brin and Larry Page, published in *Computer Networks and ISDN Systems*, 1998; and "Amazon Recommendations: Item to Item Collaborative Filtering" by Greg Linden, Brent Smith, and Jeremy York, January–February 2003, IEEE Internet Computing. We found Trefis an invaluable online resource for financial analysis about Google. We relied heavily on management consultants for an understanding of mass customization and technology. In particular, we refer to "How Digital Is Transforming Retail: The View from eBay," July 2014, published by McKinsey online; "How Technology Can Drive the Next Wave of Mass Customization" by Anshuk Gandhi, Carmen Magar, and Roger Roberts, published by McKinsey online, February 2014; and "Making It Personal: Rules for Success in Product Customization" by Elizabeth Spaulding and Christopher Perr, Bain brief, September 16, 2013. For information about changes to JetBlue products, we relied on its website and press releases as well as *Wikipedia*. For insight and data on 3-D printing, we relied on the following articles: "3D Printing: From Racing Cars to Dresses to Human Tissue" by Fiona Graham, BBC, September 8, 2014; and "On the Fast Track to Routine 3-D Printing" by Nick Bilton, the *New York Times*, February 17, 2013.

Chapter 6

We discovered the Mayo Clinic diet program after searching for information about sepsis and clicking on an article about sepsis on the Mayo Clinic website. The Mayo Clinic diet button kept popping up on the screen and we clicked through all the steps to see what would happen. We went through all the steps until it asked for our credit card. The information about the CVS Extra Care rewards program was found on the company's website in the fine print. For data on checking accounts, we relied on WalletHub's "2014 Checking Account Cost Comparison Report" by Alina Comoreanu, as well as "Checking Account Transparency Report: How Easily Can Consumers Shop for a Checking Account Online?" by the same analyst. We also quote findings from a report from the Consumer Financial Protection Bureau titled *Data Point: Checking Account Overdraft*," published July 2014, and a September 2014 survey on bank accounts by Bankrate. Information about airline tickets and frequent-flier programs came from a variety of sources, including Cwsi.net, a site dedicated to helping frequent fliers; an article in *USA Today*, "Why Can't Airline Tickets Be Transferable?" by Christopher Elliot, published December 23, 2013; and "Qantas Frequent Flyer Changes 'Bewildering' for Customers," published in the *Australian Financial Review*, September 22, 2014. The cost of a smartphone in the United States versus the United Kingdom was original reporting by Anna Bernasek and later appeared in the *New York Times* as "Two Countries, Two Vastly Different Phone Bills," August 23, 2014. We relied on a report by the U.K. regulator Ofcom titled *Cost and Value of Communications Services in the UK*, published January 2014. In terms of unexpected medical bills, we found the *New York Times* series "Paying till It Hurts" incredibly valuable and, in particular, refer to an article in the series by Elisabeth Rosenthal, "After Surgery, Surprise $117,000 Medical Bill from Doctor He Didn't Know," published September 20, 2014. We also refer to a study published September 15, 2014, by the Center for Public Policy Priorities, *Surprise Medical Bills Take Advantage of Texans: Little Known Practice Creates a 'Second Emergency' for ER Patients.*

Chapter 7

For the history of San Francisco and our population figures, we relied on data compiled by the Virtual Museum of the City of San Francisco and SFgenealogy.com. The cumulative total gold production from California stood at 118 million ounces by 2001, according to Dan Hausel's "California— Gold, Geology and Prospecting" dated February 12, 2010, citing earlier sources. Ashburn, Virginia, was covered in a *Washington Post* story "After Dramatic Growth, Ashburn Expects Even More Data Centers" on August 27, 2011. The website Data Center Knowledge presents a wealth of information on the subject, including, in particular, "Equinix Plans 1 Million Square Foot Data Center Campus in Ashburn," dated March 17, 2014; and "Estimate: Amazon Cloud Backed by 450,000 Servers," dated March 14, 2012. General information about Aldo Manuzio, who in addition to developing an early mail-order catalog also invented italic type, is available from *Wikipedia* as well as many other sources. The U.S. Federal Trade Commission published an informative report about the data-broker industry in May 2014. Amazon Web Services describes its operations on its website. The practice of requiring employees to maintain the confidentiality of company information is common, and in the case of Amazon, was referred to in a *Seattle Times* article "Amazon Sues After Ex-Worker Takes Google Job" on July 1, 2014. Detailed financial statistics and business descriptions of the "Ten" leading companies in big data are available on the U.S. Securities and Exchange website. Cited company figures are accurate as of December 31, 2014. The *Inc.* magazine story of the single mother fired for her salacious blog "Nonprofit Fires Woman for Blogging About Sex" was published May 4, 2010. John Battelle's book *The Search: How Google and Its Rivals Rewrote the Rules of Business and Transformed Our Culture* was published by Portfolio, part of Penguin Group, in 2005.

Chapter 8

Kayak searches do not include Southwest Airlines because Southwest does not share fare data with Kayak. *Wikipedia* provides a general overview of the Boston Tea Party as well as the East India Company and the history of monopolies. *Wikipedia* also covers the history of the petroleum industry. For a brief comparison of United States to U.K. real-estate costs, see the *New York Times*, "An Extra Cost in Home Sales," October 25, 2014. The *New York Times* report concerning George H. W. Bush's 1992 campaign stop at a retailer's conference is still controversial; some believe that President Bush was unfairly characterized. There is a large literature relating to antitrust and its enforcement. Robert Bork's 1978 book *The Antitrust Paradox* maintained that some types of price discrimination and other seemingly prohibited practices are beneficial to consumers. Bork's book is among the most cited works in the field.

Chapter 9

Wikipedia provides useful background on the history of the environmental movement, as does The American Experience, "Timeline: The Modern Environmental Movement" on pbs.org. Andrea Vesalius and Copernicus are seminal figures in the history of modern science. *Wikipedia* and other sources provide useful background on the history of science. The U.S. Census Bureau estimated in 2010 that 52 percent of the world's population was under the age of thirty. The Chicago River is now home to some seventy species of fish, some of which are fished. London's famous pea-soup smogs have largely abated, tamed by the legislation that followed the "great smog" of 1952 that killed 4,000 people. Published in 1949, George Orwell's *1984* was an effective fictional treatment of the social and political impact of mass surveillance and mass communication, but it largely avoided discussion of commercial and economic effects. After first appearing in *Electronics* magazine in 1965, Moore's Law was revised to its current form in 1975. See Schaller, "The Origin, Nature, and Implications of 'MOORE'S LAW,'" September 26, 1996.

Chapter 10

Google Flu Trends' initial report was published in *Nature* magazine, "Detecting Influenza Epidemics Using Search Engine Query Data" on February 19, 2009. The Beckenstein bound was formulated by Jacob D. Bekenstein. See, for example, "Universal Upper Bound on the Entropy-to-Energy Ratio for Bounded Systems," *Physical Review D*, vol. 23, no. 2, January 15, 1981. Tor's website provides an overview of its privacy features (www.torproject.org). The right to privacy was convincingly argued in an influential *Harvard Law Review* article "The Right to Privacy," dated December 15, 1890, by Samuel Warren and Louis Brandeis.

Index

Credit: Josh Lehrer Photography

ANNA BERNASEK writes the "Datapoints" column for the *New York Times* and is a writer for *Newsweek*. She has covered economics and business as a journalist and author for more than twenty years, in outlets such as *Fortune* and *Time* magazine.

D. T. MONGAN is a lawyer based in New York, specializing in finance and corporate transactions.

NATION
BOOKS

The Nation Institute

Founded in 2000, **Nation Books** has become a leading voice in American independent publishing. The inspiration for the imprint came from the *Nation* magazine, the oldest independent and continuously published weekly magazine of politics and culture in the United States.

The imprint's mission is to produce authoritative books that break new ground and shed light on current social and political issues. We publish established authors who are leaders in their area of expertise, and endeavor to cultivate a new generation of emerging and talented writers. With each of our books we aim to positively affect cultural and political discourse.

Nation Books is a project of The Nation Institute, a nonprofit media center dedicated to strengthening the independent press and advancing social justice and civil rights. The Nation Institute is home to a dynamic range of programs: the award-winning Investigative Fund, which supports ground-breaking investigative journalism; the widely read and syndicated website TomDispatch; the Victor S. Navasky Internship Program in conjunction with the *Nation* magazine; and Journalism Fellowships that support up to 25 high-profile reporters every year.

For more information on Nation Books, The Nation Institute, and the *Nation* magazine, please visit:

www.nationbooks.org

www.nationinstitute.org

www.thenation.com

www.facebook.com/nationbooks.ny

Twitter: @nationbooks